**Careers
in
Fashion**

Careers
in
Fashion

Carole Chester

Kogan
Page

First published 1984 by Kogan Page Ltd
120 Pentonville Road, London N1 9JN

Copyright © Kogan Page Ltd 1984

British Library Cataloguing in Publication Data

Chester, Carole
  Careers in fashion.
  1. Fashion — Vocational guidance —
  Great Britain
  I. Title
  746.9'2'02341   TT507

  ISBN 0-85038-828-7 (Hb)
  ISBN 0-85038-829-5 (Pb)

Printed and bound in Great Britain by
The Camelot Press Ltd, Southampton

Contents

Part 2

Part 1

Chapter 1
Introduction

Yves St Laurent, Courrèges, Balmain are all fashion names. People who buy their clothes can afford the best fabrics and workmanship and because they are often rich trend-setters who frequently appear in the media, others wish to imitate them. This makes the designers even more fashion-able, and their labels even more desirable.

Mary Quant and Laura Ashley — though less exclusive — are fashion names too, for fashion starts with an idea that people like enough to take up. It may be an idea that is shocking, exciting, provocative or just different. But if it becomes all the rage, it is 'in'. And it doesn't need to have a name behind it because a 'trend' or 'look' is often adapted to please a mass market.

Fashion is not only dress, but where you live, where you shop, where you eat, what sheets you put on your bed, what you order to drink. It may be a colour, a material, a style of make-up or hair. And it comes in 'waves', often as a reaction to the economic climate, or as a result of some topical situation. For example, the flapper dresses of the twenties expressing gaiety after the First World War, were followed by the longer, more elegant styles of the thirties, which then turned to shorter dresses in the forties when there was a shortage of material.

Though most people would agree that fashion starts with design, it needs more than a good design to get its message across. Of prime importance is publicity. Without the models to wear it, the photographers to photograph it, and the writers to tell the world about it, fashion wouldn't exist. It needs people to turn abstraction into reality —

to create patterns from drawings, and garments from patterns. Fashion has to be presented to the public in places where it may be bought. Fashion has to be sold.

It is an industry because it *does* have so many facets and each facet is important in its own right. Salary expectations, of course, vary with each aspect, but it is one industry where the sky's the limit. It is an industry, too, where there may be worthwhile perks such as travel or purchase discounts. Most of all, because it is so changeable it can offer great excitement.

Do You Have Fashion Flair?

Do you instinctively put the 'right' clothes together regardless of budget? Combine colours in an effective way? Wear clothes in such a way that friends say it's 'your' style? Can you mentally visualise colour shades and tones? Adapt a 'look' you see in a magazine to suit your own shape and personality without losing its fashionable side? Do you recognise a perfect fit? Would you know when an extra nip or tuck would improve a garment — and where to put them? If you answer 'yes' to most of these points, then you have fashion flair.

Naturally for someone to want to be part of the fashion industry, he/she must be interested in fashion. This is essential before you even ask yourself which sector you might be best equipped to handle, or which might be most beneficial in terms of actual job opportunities. If you don't already have an avid interest in clothes (and that includes writing about them), you should close this book now.

Which Sector for You?

Here are two examples of people who had a choice to make in fashion. Janet Guthrie, on the strength of her arts subjects, won a scholarship to the Royal College of Art. She was wearing quilted jackets (which she made) long before they were a fashion trend. She certainly had fashion flair, but she didn't turn into a dress designer, nor indeed into a dressmaker. Instead, she used her creative ability and artistic intuition, her training and knowledge to work in the field of ceramics. This writer was one of the first to adopt the mini and micro-mini fashions of the sixties, plus the stars on the cheeks and under the eyes of the seventies. That demonstrated fashion awareness, yet, as a writer, her main subject is not in fact fashion.

Possessing a fashion sense does not mean that you will automatically become a fashion expert — though without it you will not go far. On the other hand, just because you cannot draw or paint, this does not mean you should rule out fashion as a career. If you can, you may be better off as an illustrator, copying created lines rather than creating them yourself in the first place.

None of the sales areas of fashion (PR, marketing, copy-writing, merchandising, buying, floor selling) require winning ways with pencils and brushes. They all involve projecting somebody else's idea, albeit *in a creative way*. If you work in this area, you will be given a brief but it is how you interpret it that will make or break your career.

Let us look at a basic fashion project from different aspects of the industry: the little black dress of 1983. The designer might have in mind, for it, a topical celebrity and perhaps a new or less familiar fabric. A manufacturer might change the fabric or temper adornment to cut costs for mass production. A publicist might take advantage of either — price and/or novelty. The photographer tries to capture a mood regardless of either and the fashion writer makes a selection, more often than not, based on what can be said about the garment. A store buyer buys *en masse* with a view to profit — perhaps choosing only one item for display purposes and excitement value but more of what will sell to the store's average customer. The window-dresser adds accessory contrast or highlights the garment by clever placement. By using words with finesse, the advertising agency tries to ensure that that particular item appeals to a particular market. And so each plays a role in the ultimate goal — selling the goods.

Test Yourself

Fashion itself doesn't always have to be practical, but you who are thinking about a career in the industry, do. For instance, perhaps you have dreamed up a fantastic fur jacket creation; you draw well and it looks good on paper, but is it possible, and practical, to make? If you knew something about skins before you put pen to paper, you might have had second thoughts about your original design.

You've been given a pattern and some material and told to go ahead to make the item. But do you know enough about the fabric? Will it fall as the design suggests? Will it stretch too much? Will costs increase too much to match up the material's own design once the pattern's been cut?

Perhaps you'd like to be an illustrator. Do you have an eye for detail that takes in the essence of an outfit? As an illustrator, you may have to produce a hurried sketch that says it all. Test yourself now with a one-minute sketch of a shop-window suit seen from the bus; or draw the key points of a friend's outfit – after he or she has gone.

Writers are often limited by available space. Test your descriptive powers. Close your eyes and describe in detail exactly what the person opposite is wearing. Or make an attempt at another truly effective method: describe an object in as few words as possible (without saying what it is) so that whoever you are describing it to cannot but help guess what it is (a deck-chair is a particularly good subject for this).

Test your sales and marketing ability. Choose any object and plan a three-minute demonstration in front of friends by picking out its assets and advantages and by using comparison studies with other similar items. Then take votes on whether you could have 'sold' that object. The knack to sell may be tested any time. For example, you may want to influence a friend to buy a certain book or record, or your parents to buy you a particular present. See if you can and you'll have an idea of your own ability – and just as important, you will find out whether you enjoy it.

Use other people to help you in your assessment. A

career decision is a major one so don't scorn advice from parents and teachers — both have a fairly good idea of your abilities. You could be 'a natural', either with your hands, or at sales. You could well have 'an eye for' colour. Beware, though, the 'you're pretty enough to be a model' type of suggestion: many girls fantasise about being a model but very few make it to the top. Having a beautiful face is not enough, and a number of girls who are pretty in the flesh simply don't photograph well enough (see Chapter 7).

Qualifications

Theoretically, traditional academic qualifications are not necessary for entry into some areas of the fashion industry. After all, a degree in Classics will not help the photographer with photography, nor a would-be model with her camera appeal. A shop assistant's science degree would be wasted and a seamstress doesn't have to be able to write a brilliant composition.

However, if you plan to study art and design, journalism, marketing or related subjects, you will certainly need some O levels (and often a minimum of two As) to be accepted for any degree or training course.

Which Course?

There is a bewildering variety of courses available in fashion-related areas, although only the London College of Fashion offers training in all the main fields. These are:

- ☐ foundation courses
- ☐ vocational courses
- ☐ degree courses
- ☐ CNAA degree courses
- ☐ diploma of higher education courses
- ☐ postgraduate courses
- ☐ certificate and diploma courses
- ☐ sandwich or part-time courses.

Foundation Courses

Before taking a degree course in art and design, students are expected to have completed a one- or two-year foundation course which gives them a broader, preparatory education before specialising. Because it involves working with a variety of materials and subjects, it also helps students to make that final specialist decision.

School-leavers aged 16 can take the two-year course if they have at least three O levels, and preferably more. Minimum age for the one-year course is 17 with at least five O levels (plus, preferably, one A level or more).

To apply for a foundation course, write directly to the college which interests you (a list of available courses may be obtained from your local education authority). You will probably be called for an interview and asked to bring a portfolio of your work. Normally you will be asked to state your preference of subject before you start, even though you will cover several subjects which may lead you later to change your mind. The main reason for this is so that you have time to prepare an appropriate portfolio for application to a subsequent CNAA degree or vocational course. But do remember: completion of a foundation course does not automatically mean a place for the latter two courses.

Note: If planning a career in advertising, marketing or public relations, a CAM (Communication Advertising and Marketing Education Foundation Ltd) foundation course is recommended. It may be taken part-time over a one- or two-year period. (See Certificate and Diploma Courses below.)

Vocational Courses

If you feel you're not academically up to a degree course, but wish to pursue art and design as a career — or indeed other areas of the fashion industry — a vocational course may be the answer, since it offers practical training. Non-degree students are likely to attend a vocational course locally for anything from one to four years.

Students of 16 are expected to have a general education

but some advanced courses are designed for 18-year-olds with at least five O levels. Most colleges will require completion of a foundation course (see above). However, since entry requirements vary so much at present, until the Business and Technician Education Council (BTEC) standardises them you should check with the college concerned. At the moment, vocational courses lead to certificates, diplomas, higher diplomas or regional awards.

Degree Courses

If you are academically minded, a university degree provides both a higher education and the experience of being a full-time student. Normally, you'll take a three-year course leading to a BA though some four-year sandwich courses exist in which you would spend one year in employment in an area related to your studies.

Minimum requirements are five GCE passes including two at A level. For an arts degree, a university may stipulate one of the A level subjects as art, or art with history. For a business studies degree, an O level in mathematics is generally required.

Alternative acceptable qualifications include GCE in four subjects if three of them are at A level; a Scottish certificate of education with three or four passes at Higher level out of four or five subjects respectively. An Ordinary national certificate or diploma may stand you in good stead for some degree courses, as will a completed foundation course together with five O levels or four Os and one A.

Note: The above are minimal requirements. Competition for acceptance into the top universities or for popular courses is exceptionally keen, so only the best-qualified school-leavers will earn a place. You must also read carefully the entrance requirements at your chosen college and make sure that you have the right ones before applying.

All university applications must go through UCCA (Universities Central Council on Admissions), except for admission to Aberdeen, Glasgow and Strathclyde, when you apply direct. Choose five universities, list them in order of preference and give details of your own qualifications on the form UCCA provides. The form also asks you to describe your hobbies and requires your school to write a confidential report about you. One or more of the chosen universities may decide to interview you personally, to offer you an unconditional place without interview, or to make a conditional offer dependent on grades. Two offers may be held at any one time.

Opening date for applications is 1 September. Closing date for Oxford and Cambridge, mid-October; for all other universities, mid-December. Secondary applications may be made after January for courses still open. The *UCCA Handbook* sets out full application details.

Remember that degree courses are also offered by some colleges of higher education, arts colleges and polytechnics.

CNAA Degree Courses

These are available at polytechnics, art colleges, some colleges of higher education and other institutions, and are more practical in content than a university degree course. Many colleges plan their own syllabuses and exams – both of which are vetted and approved by the Council for National Academic Awards. Some rely on overall assessment rather than on one final exam to award a degree. Some allow students to choose their own programme from a wide available range.

Minimum age is generally 18, after completion of a foundation course. Minimum academic requirements are five GCE O levels, three Os plus one A, or two Os and two As. Scottish equivalents are also accepted. Those who haven't taken a foundation course need at least two GCE A levels plus some Os, or other qualifications such as ONC/OND, HNC/HND and BTEC diplomas and certificates.

Stiff competition may mean that some institutions require more academic achievements. Always check with the ones you are interested in. All applications for degree courses (except to Scottish colleges) must be made through the Art Design and Admissions Registry (ADAR), Imperial Chambers, 24 Widemarsh Street, Hereford HR4 9EO.

Diploma of Higher Education Courses

If you're unsure about your area of study, this two-year course gives you the time to come to a decision without wasting time towards a degree, for whilst a qualification in its own right, the DipHE also leads to degrees or professional qualifications. Courses are offered by polytechnics, colleges of higher education and some universities. Usual entry requirement is two GCE A levels. After passing the exam at the end of two years, you may opt to transfer to the third year of a degree course.

Postgraduate Courses

Think carefully before taking on postgraduate work so far as the field of fashion is concerned, as it will add on another one to three years of perhaps unnecessary further education. Advance courses are available in a wide range of subjects and lead to certificates, diplomas and higher degrees such as an MA. The usual entry requirement is the completion of a first degree, though vocational and professional qualifications may be acceptable in some cases.

Certificate and Diploma Courses

If the business/marketing end of fashion is where you think your skills lie, you could consider a Business and Technician Education Council (BTEC) certificate or diploma course. The former takes two years part-time; the latter, one year full-time. A national certificate course takes two years part-time; a diploma course, two years full-time. Option subjects include 'introduction to marketing' and 'principles of buying'.

The CAM certificate takes two years part-time and all six subjects (marketing, advertising, public relations, media, research and behavioural studies, communication practice) must be passed in order to qualify. The diploma takes one year part-time in three specialist areas: advertising and marketing, media and public relations. Students choose their own methods of study: correspondence courses, evening classes or full-time.

An Institute of Marketing certificate course takes two years part-time; the diploma course, one year part-time. The latter may only be taken upon successful completion of the former. Courses are offered by some further education colleges, polytechnics and correspondence colleges.

Diplomas and certificates are awarded at many colleges specialising in advertising, film-making, journalism, marketing, graphic design, fashion design, tailoring etc, after successful completion of a course.

Part-Time and Sandwich Courses

Both of these are combined with employment. A sandwich course is literally 'sandwiched' between periods of employment. This might mean two years of study, one year of work experience, and a final year of study (as is the case at some universities). It may mean six months of study, and six months of work.

Evening courses in dressmaking, drawing, business studies, etc are available throughout the country. Find out where and when from your local reference library or education office. Though they rarely lead to a qualification, they may aid a career decision or give added help to existing studies.

Grants

Grants may be given in two forms: discretionary or mandatory. In the first instance, there is no obligation for the local education authority concerned to grant you an award, and if it does the amount may vary. In the second instance, the authority is obliged to give a major grant, assuming you are eligible. In Scotland grants are paid through the Education Department. A full grant covers tuition fees, college dues, student union fees plus an allowance for board and lodging, books and necessary equipment. Full details are available in the DES leaflet, *Grants for*

Students, a Brief Guide — free from DES Information Division, Elizabeth House, York Road, London SE1. Scottish applicants should write to St Andrew's House, Edinburgh.

Grants are, of course, dependent upon your parents' financial situation and many local education authorities have severely cut their budgets. Application for grants should be made a year in advance of planned courses. Basically, degree and DipHE courses involve mandatory awards; foundation and vocational courses, discretionary awards. Grants for postgraduate and higher degrees, diploma and certificate courses are also discretionary.

Chapter 2
History of Fashion

Dress styles of yesteryear are particularly important to the design student, for they can be — and have been — inspirational in the creation of new trends. Fashions are also influenced by the introduction of new manufacturing techniques and fabrics. And then each era of civilisation (eg Greek, Roman, Egyptian) has made its mark on designs of later periods.

All kinds of things have affected modes of dress — Christianity brought in conservatism, whilst travel gave rise to new ideas. For example, the Crusaders returning from the East in the thirteenth century brought back fine embroidered accessories, creating a new vogue to be copied. It is interesting to note that as long ago as the thirteenth century, Paris was showing so much fashion flair that soon Venice (then at the height of its prosperity) was importing every year a French fashion doll dressed in the latest style — a sort of fashion journalism that lasted for years.

Lace, an evolution of embroidery, appeared in Italy and Flanders about the middle of the sixteenth century and soon became a highly prized form of trimming. In England, during the reign of Mary I, only those with status higher than a baron were allowed to wear 'lace ruffles'. From history, we learn that the hoop skirt came to France in 1530 with Eleanor of Castile, the second wife of François I, and that it grew to exaggerated proportions in the reign of Elizabeth I. Catherine de Medici, wife of Henri II, is said to have brought the steel corset to France, and this was certainly a key feature of the mode of Elizabeth's time. And we learn that Mary Stuart and Catherine de Medici were the first to wear shoes with 'high heels'.

Like them, Elizabeth wore what became known as 'pumps' and she is said to have been the first English-woman to wear silk stockings. (Silk was the most expensive and luxurious foreign material, available in this era only to the very wealthy. The major English product was wool.) Hand-knitting was introduced into Britain in the same century and, in 1589, William Lee invented a knitting-machine for stockings only to be ignored by Court — and so he settled in France instead. After his death in 1610, his brother returned to England, to Nottingham, where framework knitters joined together to form a trade association. Later on, other items such as gloves started being produced.

The Louis XIII period is important because it was at that time that France established herself without doubt as arbiter of the mode. Ribbon became fashionable; the doublet became a waistcoat with sleeves; and the cravat appeared for the first time. England under James I and Charles I simply followed suit. It was the age of the 'cavalier' look, when men wore plumes in their hats and there was a vogue for white — whether silk, cloth or velvet. (During this era was the first mention of an all-white wedding-dress, when Princess Elizabeth married the Prince Palatine.)

Key features of the period included the 'Van Dyck collar' and bunches of ribbon loops on different parts of a costume. The smart male world wore pearl earrings and jewelled buttons whilst women adopted the pre-runner of 'pinafores' — fashionable, beautifully worked aprons called 'pinners'.

This period provides a good illustration of how politics (or current situation) can affect fashion, for the Puritans under Cromwell scorned the fripperies of the cavalier costume. Though they didn't create a style, they sobered the colours and rejected trimmings.

Not surprisingly, when Charles II regained the throne, he brought Louis XIV fashions with him: masses of ribbons; a short jacket with short sleeves showing a full, sheer lace-trimmed shirt whose full sleeves were tied with ribbons.

The 'jack boot' appeared in 1665 — a rigid leather boot for hard wear — and a 'coat and vest' followed Paris trends. Women wore mantuas — not unlike kimonos — copying their French cousins, laced their corsets more tightly creating a slimmer figure, and started wearing a riding habit — a long-skirted, buttoned-up coat worn over a sidesaddle skirt.

Fashion itself led to technical achievements. In order to cut down the import of Indian printed cottons, there were experiments to produce similar material in England whilst new machines turned raw silk into organza. By the eighteenth century, many more techniques were perfected and new inventions included the spinning-jenny, devised in 1741.

Increased travel in the eighteenth century meant quicker fashion changes and more refinements. Lighter materials were used, but an element of formality was introduced. The frock-coat came in and so did the shawl. The short-waisted jacket called a 'Spencer' (invented by Lord Spencer) was used by men and women and English children were the first to wear unrestrictive clothing. There were innovations in underwear, too, like the wearing of 'drawers', an original French fashion that became generally acceptable around the 1830s.

English tailors led the field in men's fashion. With their long experience in working with wool, they gave clothes distinctive elegance, and the invention of the tape measure helped 'line'. One of the important coats to appear in the 1850s was the 'Raglan'. The wide sleeves which have since become fashionable time and time again, were a practicality for the man after whom it was named — Lord Henry Raglan, who lost an arm in the Crimean War. The forerunner of the Ascot tie began to be worn and shirt collars and cuffs became detachable.

Women, who had worn many petticoats under widening skirts, replaced them with the crinoline hoop and, later, with the bustle (1860). The 'Princess' dress appeared in the sixties — one piece from neck to hem with buttons or bows down the centre. The 'jacket and skirt' costume became popular, complete with tightly buttoned waistcoat and a narrow bow tie to the blouse. The hat replaced bonnets and caps, particularly the 'pork pie' style. And the invention of the sewing-machine made a notable impact on all dressmaking.

You will recognise many style names from the Victorian period: the dinner-coat, for instance, a dress-coat without tails which was first seen in England in the 1880s, was called a 'tuxedo' in America; the separate shirt front of the thirties — the 'dickey'; and the 'Norfolk jacket' of heavy tweed, named for the Duke of Norfolk. The 'Chesterfield' overcoat, which became a twentieth century classic, was first worn in this era which also saw the first bowler. Indeed, when the machine to manufacture felt was invented in 1846, it brought in many new hat styles. British stylists also turned soft felt hats of German and Austrian origin into 'homburgs' and 'fedoras'. The latter style was worn by both sexes in the eighties and nineties. Another machine, perfected for sewing straw in 1870, made the 'boater' possible.

Costume became far more specialised: a mode of dress for day and one for evening; for city living and for country visits; for sporting occasions such as cycling, golf or yachting — all of which required more practical clothing design.

What of the twentieth century? By the start of it, men's clothing had become standardised. Cut, shape, length and breadth changed, and continue to do so, but not greatly. The first decade saw the padded shoulder, and also the decline of it in 1910 in favour of the more conservative natural shoulderline. In the twenties, the straight-backed short jacket was a minor revolution against the nipped-in waist. The thirties brought the 'drape' idea through which good tailoring could seemingly add height to a short man and slim down one who was fat.

Designers tried to add fullness to trousers, but weren't successful until the 'Oxford bags' of the twenties which were sometimes as wide as 24 inches at the bottom. Gradually, they tapered down again and pleats at the waist were an early thirties' fashion. The wide knickerbockers of the twenties, for sports purposes, became known as 'plus fours' — a term straight from the British army when breeches were measured as reaching to the knees, plus four inches.

The white mess-jacket, worn with a cummerbund, not a waistcoat, was the dressy vogue of the thirties, followed by the white dinner-jacket, all the more popular in chic Caribbean and Florida resorts. For informal occasions, Harris tweed was in great demand in the first half of this century and the 'polo-coat' became a key fashion note, along with the 'polo-shirt'.

Synthetics have been perhaps the most noticeable fashion addition so that, after the First World War, suits in wool, gabardine, seersucker etc were popular for summer wear, especially in America, and synthetic fabrics replaced silk for linings. Water-repellent cloth was a further innovation, attested by the raincoat and then the trench coat.

Style changes for women were far more perceptible, though again they have been repeated — for example, the 'Bishop sleeve' of 1903, the dropped shoulderline and the kimono sleeve; the 'straightening' of skirts with the 'Empire' line of 1910 (tubelike and trainless) and, later, the 'hobble skirt'. 'Dolman sleeves' were revived for coats and crocheted fashions were 'in'. With the coming of the motor car, long coats, and hats with yards of chiffon veil to tie them (so they wouldn't fall off whilst riding in an open car) became *de rigueur* for the well-dressed lady.

'Harem trousers' met with no more success in 1912 than they have recently but the short full skirt (8 inches from the ground) made famous by Lanvin, did. As we know, the twenties' flappers loved the knee-length versions of the chemise (at its shortest around 1925). Chanel introduced jersey to make chemises in 1918. The new look needed very little corseting — indeed, one said goodbye to figure curves and yearned for a boyish silhouette with little bosom. Petticoats disappeared and silk slips were worn only when necessary.

The short skirt length produced a change in footwear — to the 'baby Louis' heel, intricate straps and lots of ornaments. Only in 1930 did the hemline start to descend again, and the beltline (which had been at hip level) began to creep up to its normal place. Feathers, gold and silver turbans and beadwork were in great demand for evening wear. The 'little black dress' became a standard wardrobe requisite and the cloche was a popular hat. The beret was another style of small hat which took firm hold.

The thirties offered all kinds of silhouette options, from bouffant or slim-skirted evening gowns to the broad, square-shouldered tailored clothes for day wear. The halter-dress, the dinner-dress with accompanying jacket, and the evening-sweater were all launched. In 1939, a touch of daring showed dresses with a bare midriff; the 'shirtwaist' made one item from blouse and skirt; and shoes were spike-heeled and open-toed.

Curvaceous women breathed with relief after the Second World War and the hour-glass silhouette returned. Wasp-belts were in (to make the waist small); waist-length brassieres helped shape a tight bodice and strapless bras coped with the fashion for bare shoulders. Dior's circular skirt called for the wearing of several petticoats at one time, often in different-coloured, flounced taffetas. The 'ballet-length' cocktail-dress moved into the cocktail-hour picture and skirts in general lengthened, once the need to save on fabric had been eased.

The ups and downs of fashion never cease. We have seen British designers in the sixties make one of the biggest impacts on the world with their mini and micro-mini skirts, but they only achieved a mild reactivated influence in the eighties with what has been termed the 'ra-ra' skirt. Dr Zhivago coats have swept into the fashion pages while the calf-length midi swept out, mostly unsold. Films, not to mention widespread tourism, have inspired the 'peasant' look — Indian, Cossack and Arabian Nights attire. We have watched men's and women's clothes made and labelled 'unisex' and sportswear become briefer.

If you are interested in studying fashion history, your

local library reference section is a good place to begin. Once you have started on a design course and found a lecturer to sponsor you, you may apply for a ticket to use the library at the Victoria and Albert Museum or the British Library. Two other costume libraries which take students by appointment are the Fashion Research Centre in Bath and the Gallery of English Costume in Manchester. There are, however, more than 120 museums and galleries in the UK which collect costume. The *ABC Guide to Museums and Art Galleries*, published annually, gives a short entry for each museum, arranged by county.

Chapter 3
Career Expectations

To give positive career expectations in the world of fashion is like saying how long is a piece of string. Did the Emanuels know they would become so famous . . . and so rich . . . when they were design students? Did Lord Beaverbrook ever realise he would own a newspaper empire, when he was a small boy in Canada? Was it luck or judgement that made Ruder & Finn internationally known in the field of advertising?

The common denominator is that they all strove for success; they hoped for the top, reached out towards it and worked extremely hard. Not everyone can reach the top of their chosen career, and even if they do, it's a precarious position to keep. But it shouldn't stop you from trying.

Career expectations depend upon variables: individual talent, qualifications, being in the right place at the right time. A combination of knowledge plus luck, judgement plus creativity, making the right job move at the right time when given an opportunity out of the blue are all factors in career success.

Which Area is Most Lucrative?

A very hard question to answer. A fashion editor for a national newspaper, a fashion photographer working for 'the glossies', a top model, a marketing consultant, a fashion designer with his/her own label, a senior advertising account executive — all may earn thousands of pounds a year. In addition, they receive perks such as overseas travel and expense account meals. But there aren't too many people in fashion's top bracket, although there are plenty in the running.

That First Job

It's the hardest! Your own college careers office should be able to give you initial help, but you'll need to study the job advertisements in as many papers as possible. Don't be afraid of applying to however many you think may suit your background. Buy specialist magazines which specifically list vacancies in the design, media and marketing fields, for example *UK Press Gazette*, *Marketing Week*, *Campaign*. Don't expect the first job to be wonderful. Swallow your pride and be glad to be given a junior position: if you're good, promotion will come quickly.

Pick out some of the major companies whose products or services interest you and write to their personnel department whilst you are still taking a course. Though they may have no vacancies at that particular moment, it doesn't hurt to be on their files and if you check again when you've completed your course, you may find they have a job for you.

Trainees

Many large companies and some major advertising agencies operate management trainee schemes which may or may not include day-release to study for formal or further qualifications. For the first few months, the trainee will learn about the company as a whole, spending some time in each department before being assigned to a specific section. Your school or college careers office, or the local authority careers service should be able to advise you on regional availability.

Press photographers and journalism trainees usually work with local and provincial newspapers through an NUJ apprenticeship scheme.

If you have taken a course for a professional qualification, the professional body concerned may well be able to offer job advice relevant to that field. (Minimum entry for these courses is agreed upon between colleges and professional associations. It may mean an extra year on top of your chosen course. You may have to take an additional, special exam, or it may give you automatic entry after you've finished your course.)

Some of the useful associations are: Society of Industrial Artists and Designers; Communication Advertising and Marketing Foundation Ltd; Associateship of the Textile Institute; British Institute of Professional Photography, Association of Illustrators; Institute of Practitioners in Advertising.

Promotion

It is possible to anticipate some promotion ladders. The student who starts off as an assistant buyer in a medium-sized store can expect to move up to buyer and then, perhaps, transfer to a position in a large store or chain buying-office. Sometimes the job title doesn't change, but the responsibility and salary do; for example, a buyer for a smallish department might be moved to a far larger department. A career in buying may also eventually lead to store management.

The junior copywriter can move up to a senior position and perhaps reach that of account executive for a major fashion account. The management trainee interested in marketing may become marketing manager, marketing director and, possibly, even achieve the title 'vice-president of marketing' or open his/her own consultancy.

A needlewoman/seamstress involved in working on mass-produced garments is unlikely to move far. However, a knowledge of dressmaking, combined with design, is necessary for both the clothes designer headed for the top, and the manufacturer. It is also essential for costume design for film, theatre or TV. Textile knowledge is important to all these careers though young textile students may move directly into a textile manufacturing company that is constantly on the lookout for fresh talent.

More than likely, the young would-be fashion writer will start off his/her career writing up weddings and obituaries for a local paper before covering more interesting subjects. One of the advantages of local, provincial papers is that there are few people, writing about many topics, so that fashion could well become one of your special subjects. Once you have become fashion editor or Women's Page editor of a local paper, then is the time to look for a similar position on a national or magazine.

It is still true that one way of getting into journalism and public relations is via the secretarial route — but it may be a slow one. Usually, it happens when the boss is overworked, the secretary shows flair and interest and is therefore then given the opportunity to do small things to help out.

Often a journalist will sidestep into public relations, mainly because it is usually better paid and requires a knowledge of writing. A student of PR might start at a fairly low level in a small or large agency and gradually be given more client responsibility, or move 'in house' within a large company with a PR department. As a general rule, a PR officer has a more important role than a press officer because the former's job involves marketing, sometimes advertising, and often a liaison factor with more than just the press.

Freelance Possibilities

For the young photographer or illustrator, going freelance (at least at first) may be the only way to earn money. You could start soliciting work whilst still studying, hope that art directors will be among the visitors to the end-of-course degree or diploma show, or make the rounds of art directors, publishers, advertising agencies and design studios when you are out of college.

An illustrator must always take a portfolio and be persistent. Full-time jobs are available but you're more likely to be commissioned on a freelance basis to start with. Seek practical advice from your college staff and any established illustrators you know. Don't be afraid of asking for recommendations from potential employers. The Association of Illustrators also has an advisory service and a regular newsletter covering all aspects of freelance illustrating.

The newly qualified photographer can make an approach in the same way — prepare a portfolio and make the rounds of magazine art directors, advertising agencies and photographic studios, in the hope of commissions. A college-leaver might find full-time employment as a photographic assistant but competition is tough.

Similarly, a fashion designer may approach clothing and textile manufacturers with ideas and designs, seeking commissions. You might equally be able to design and produce your own original garments and sell them on a small scale and, if you are successful at this, you may well be offered a full-time job with a large manufacturer.

To become a professional freelance writer, it usually works the other way round — first you must establish yourself in the field and then go freelance. This is especially true for a specialist subject like fashion, though less true for news or feature ideas.

Chapter 4
Wholesale Career Areas

For guidance purposes, this book divides the fashion industry into two career areas: wholesale and retail. Basically, the wholesale area is concerned with the *making* of fashions and the retail with *selling* them.

The wholesale division requires technical knowledge, sometimes highly specialised, for example, work with leather or fur. Overall, it is perhaps the more practical of the two areas. Wholesaling means dealing with the trade as opposed to the public; fashion at its 'nitty gritty'.

To produce one garment may involve several sectors of the industry. A simple dress, for example, may call for ribbon or lace trim; buttons made of plastic, or metal-based; a plastic or leather belt with perhaps a metal buckle. A pair of shoes or hat might need ribbon bows or metal adornments. A leather jacket may be designed with knitted inserts.

How Wholesaling Works

Since wholesaling is concerned with practical matters, the courses you take should be related: how to sew, how to work a knitting-machine, how to cut leather or stitch fur. There is a wide range of design options from dress and footwear design to textiles. If you are considering owning or at least managing a wholesale fashion house, be sure to take a course that includes some business administration.

A wholesaler may also be an importer, or buy from one. Some furriers, for example, import skins direct from America or Scandinavia to be made up in their own workrooms in England. Some buy skins from reputable import houses and some have garments made at source and import them completed.

Skilled labour is often cheaper abroad which is why a wholesaler may take designs over to somewhere like Hong Kong to be made up. (Large retailers such as Selfridges often do the same.) A wholesaling manufacturer may well prepare more prototype designs than will eventually go into the production line.

There are basically four seasons in fashion, always worked a year in advance, but in the case of swimwear or knitwear, usually only two. The designer working for a mass-market manufacturer must have a keen eye for what will appeal to the general public by picking out 'aspects' of a top couturier's line and adapting them.

Design Comes First

Unless you intend to be a cutter or machinist in the fashion industry, you do need a design course at college; however, much of the production knowledge will be acquired during your first job. Try to obtain practical experience during holiday time whilst taking the course, or even unpaid time after you've finished a course.

Expect to start off as a design assistant when you will probably help make up samples and cut patterns. In the mass-market areas, production and costing knowledge are essential. Quantities of fabric and necessary trimmings must be costed in order to produce a saleable garment, lessening the designer's scope in purist terms, but adding beneficial training for subsequent management posts.

Creative talent is important but is often only part of the production process. Management will give its design team a 'brief' and budget and the designer must stick to it. A proposed range will be created and samples made up but it will be the managers and factory who will ultimately decide on what to produce on a large scale.

Being Your Own Wholesaler

After college, you could set up your own business on a small scale by designing — and producing — garments and selling them to retailers. If you are successful, you might hire an outworker even if you're working from home, and if orders from shops flood in, think about looking for a workshop and hiring more people. Knitwear, by hand and/or machine, is one fashion area which can be profitable in this way; hand-crafted leather is another. If you are successful on your own, you may be approached after a while by a large manufacturer who wants you to work full time for them — in which case the decision is yours whether to stay small or join the mass market.

Management

A course which includes business administration and management can lead to a design manager post, to market research or, indeed, to innumerable areas in the retail sector of the industry. Fashion and textile design courses also prepare students for careers in production and/or management in the manufacturing industries.

Courses

Fashion and textile design courses may be taken at several levels of qualification: foundation, vocational, degree and postgraduate. Courses contain a variety of aspects, from general design study and professional design practice to specific techniques like weaving, printing and dyeing, pattern designing and cutting, sewing and the use of machines necessary to the fashion industry. Some, such as knitwear design or embroidery, are specialised; some include management studies such as accounting, commerce and economics.

Chapter 5
Wholesale Jobs

Fashion Designer

Whilst fashion and accessory design courses exist on all levels from diploma to degree and postgraduate, the fashion designer should have a knowledge of textile design, especially if proposing to work in a specific area such as knitwear. A basic art course followed by a foundation course is perhaps one of the best ways for the serious designer to train. A first job might be as a design assistant for a fashion house or studio team, most likely working for mass-produced ranges of garments.

College career offices may help you to find your first job, but if you are willing to work and learn (even unpaid) during your college course, you may have better opportunities. Sandwich courses automatically give you work placement periods for practical experience.

Textile design courses of use to fashion garments might include training in printed, knitted and woven textiles and perhaps embroidery, lace and trimmings. A number of textile manufacturers employ young freelance designers just out of college. Freelance designers of all kinds may become craftsmen in their own right, producing from home a limited range of items which they sell direct to local retail outlets.

Case Studies

Ann-Marie is a designer for an upmarket sportswear manufacturer making classical, elegant separates. She took a four-year sandwich BA fashion degree course at St Martin's

College specialising in design, but also including languages, journalism, promotion and business studies.

> Since there was block-release for almost a year, I had tremendous work experience — buying and designing at corporate level and working with big name designers like Zandra Rhodes. I was offered this, my first job, at the end of my degree course, after the end-of-college show. After completion of degree courses, all students show a small collection to press, buyers and industry. Every fashion college does this — it dictates the standards of that year.
>
> My present job involves designing the collection, looking after the image of the company, choosing fabrics and following through with promotion. I'm very lucky as I'm an individual here, not part of a whole team.
>
> I would suggest that any school-leaver concentrates on art and takes a foundation course to prepare him/her for a further course. The foundation course gives you time to experiment with different areas of design before consolidating your own ideas. Personally, a fashion degree course at an art college, I feel, is of far more benefit to a serious designer than a diploma from the London College of Fashion which tends to concentrate on the skills rather than pure design. A design assistant starting out can earn between £5,000 and £6,000; an average designer might get from £10,000 to £15,000 and the really top ones as much as £40,000 per annum.

Julia, after a one-year foundation course, spent three years at an art college for her diploma in art and design, specialising in theatre design.

> It helped with all-round knowledge on set design, props and costume, but I really learned more after I left and worked for a well-known theatrical costumier for two years. I then worked for the Royal Opera House, specialising in hats and head-dresses. You had to be creative — we had only small biro sketches to work from and had to make things up on our own.

Julia has since tried her hand at freelancing from her own home, making hats and selling them to local shops on a one-off basis, as well as appliqués which she sells from a market stall herself.

Sue had a very similar background and indeed was a colleague making costumes at the Royal. She now wishes to specialise in shoemaking and has apprenticed herself (for very little money) to a well-known shoemaker to learn the trade. However, she could also have taken one of the vocational courses available, which specialise in this area of fashion.

Yvonne, after her one-year foundation course, took a three-year degree course for an MA at Kingston College (recommended for fashion) and, afterwards, a three-year postgraduate course at the Royal. After an excellent degree show, she freelanced, selling her own designed and made-up garments to shops, and she is currently also selling from her own stall at Covent Garden.

Manufacturer

After completion of fashion, art and design, or clothing technology courses, it is possible to go into business on a small scale; a number of young people then sell what they have made at market stalls. To work in large-scale manufacturing, though, practical experience with a clothing concern is necessary first. But all types of manufacturers need technical knowledge so that they know whether or not a design is feasible.

Garment Technology

Learning cutting and sewing skills can lead to BTEC certificates and diplomas, or may mean taking CGLI exams. Certain courses are available for those who specifically wish to become cutters, machinists or other members of a manufacturing team. Sometimes a clothing technology course leads to a job in quality control.

Case Study

Jane took a three-year technical course at the London College of Fashion, leading to a higher BTEC diploma.

> I could have taken a four-year clothing management course, but I wanted something more practical. My first job was as an assistant garment technologist at a chain-store, moving up to a senior position which basically has a quality-control

function. The job involves constant liaising with buyers and suppliers — in my case, swimwear and underwear. You look at the garments to make sure they have been made to the right sizing and quality.

You will have first approved a sample and done several checks at the factory, so it's no inside job, though there is a lot of paperwork, too. My college course concentrated on women's light clothing. The first year gained me an ordinary diploma, the second two years, the higher one. It involved learning to design and make clothes and also how to follow things right through to production, costing and testing. An assistant technologist can expect to earn £4,500 to £5,000; a senior, up to £7,000. A background in clothing technology is also a good way to get into buying.

BTEC Awards

BTEC programmes are of a unit structure, each unit representing 75 study hours. A pass level must be obtained in each unit. The BTEC certificate comprises 12 units; the diploma, 20 units plus 4 units of industrial experience; the higher certificate, 8 units and the higher diploma, 16 units.

The BTEC awards prepare students for jobs as pattern-cutter/designer; stylist copyist; pattern cutter; sample pattern-cutter; grader; production technician; clothing-machine technician and sample machinist. The higher awards are for those who seek supervisory and junior management positions either in the sample room or production department of a clothing company.

To take a BTEC diploma course, qualifications are: age 16 with three O levels that include English and mathematics. For the higher diploma, requirements are: age 18, with five GCE passes that include one A level. If you're headed for the 'garment development' option, those subjects must include English; if the option is to be 'garment manufacture', subjects must include English and maths or science. This same qualification can lead to a college diploma in clothing management, a four-year course in two parts, leading to associateship of the Clothing and Footwear Institute (ACFI).

The Speciality Market

In many cases art and design courses, fashion or clothing technology courses include speciality options, for instance millinery or knitwear. Furriery is a little more special. The London College of Fashion features a three-year part-time day-release course which gives a general introduction to the fur industry in the first year, and follows it up with manufacturing processes plus specialist modules for nailers and cutters or finishers and machinists.

Often one of the major furriers such as Saga Furs of Scandinavia will ask fashion students to design items for their annual Design Awards scheme, which has been going on for 15 years. Finalists' designs are made up and sent around to furriers who often take on a design and put it into production.

As an example of how the scheme works, in 1982 fashion students from Kingston, Harrow and Ravensbourne Colleges were asked to compete. In 1983, fashion students from the Royal College of Art were asked to create a part of the Saga design collection. All these students had completed a three-year fashion degree course and those of the highest standard would go on to study for a further two years' postgraduate training and, ultimately, obtain an MA degree.

Chapter 6

Retail Career Areas

To retail fashion is to sell it to the general public, but that doesn't only mean exchanging money for goods received. 'Selling' jobs employ a variety of people with a range of talents that includes 'buying'. Mostly retailing is concerned with presentation and packaging — in other words, marketing.

Marketing is a newish, umbrella term for several career areas — providing a link with both manufacturer and sales person, and sometimes direct with the customer who makes the purchase. It involves research and analysis into trends; keeping an eye on competitors; product-planning and then merchandising; advertising and promotion.

The retail area may require specific knowledge such as writing or other creative abilities. Or it may simply require a sales knack. The latter may actually lead to a higher paid career in marketing and may be the ideal answer for the person who can't draw or write but enjoys meeting people and is both a good talker and listener.

How Retailing Works

Because the retail area encompasses such a wide range of possibilities, you should be aware of your ultimate aim. A would-be fashion journalist should take a basic journalism course. Similarly, a fashion photographer needs a photography course plus some practical experience. The fashion illustrator, coordinator and window-dresser will find art and design courses useful. Courses specifically for advertising or public relations are available, but both areas are covered in a marketing degree.

Let's follow a garment through its retail stages. The manufacturer has made a dress which he previews to buyers, either from stores or a buying corporation. The store buyer decides it is a dress worth promoting so the window-dresser arranges an eye-catching setting for it and the advertising department uses artists and copywriters to design an advertisement. The public relations officer (or press officer) tells the fashion press about the dress and has it photographed on a model. The press use the picture and write about it in magazines and newspapers to excite the public into buying. If the fashion department runs out of that particular dress, then the sales person must try to interest the customer in another garment.

Courses Related to Marketing

The newer universities are likely to be the best choice for a degree with a marketing, advertising or other appropriate content. Usually the courses comprise several options and may be sandwich courses where at least one out of the four years is spent in related employment.

A CNAA degree may be obtained by completing courses in polytechnics, colleges of art and design, colleges of education and higher education. Such courses tend to be more practically orientated than university degrees and are awarded on continuous assessment rather than a final exam.

A degree or vocational course may be taken in textile and fashion design. CAM certificates include marketing, advertising and public relations, among the six subjects to be passed, and require two years of part-time study. Diplomas are also awarded for these subjects after one year's part-time study.

Certificates in marketing are obtainable by taking a two-year part-time course sponsored by the Institute of Marketing, and subsequent diplomas are awarded after completion of a further one-year part-time course. Such a course may be taken at either further education colleges, polytechnics or correspondence colleges.

Are You the Right Person?

Can you easily assimilate large amounts of information from a variety of sources? Can you be highly persuasive about ideas and plans you wish to put across to other people? Are you able to see the forest as well as the trees? If the answer to all three is 'yes', then you have a good line on marketing. Are you methodical, not slap-dash? Can you also present ideas in a favourable way? Do you have a gut feeling for layout, design and its effectiveness? If so, you might consider advertising as a career. Are you imaginative and articulate? Do you speak and write well, and look good? Do you always learn something thoroughly, and not half-heartedly? Then think about public relations.

On the other hand, someone (no matter how good-looking) who doesn't photograph well will never be a cover girl model whilst someone else who is planning a fashion photo career must be aware of visual effects. If you think you can provide information and advice in an assured way, sales is for you but don't expect to be a super salesman right out of school (the kind who goes on to be corporate head of sales and vice-president sales) − it does take experience outside the academic world.

Other Course Possibilities

A course in graphic design often has specialist areas suited to the fashion industry such as illustration, or has second and third year options in advertising design, photography and film. Living as we do in a computer age, an increasing number of graphic design courses feature a knowledge of cinema, TV and video. Courses are available at degree, vocational and foundation level.

Whilst film, photography and TV often appear as supporting studies, they also exist as degree and vocational courses in their own right. A diploma in photography with the British Institute of Professional Photography is likely to stress techniques and theory. On the other hand, a fine arts course may still have photography as a main area, but creativity comes first, and technical studies are minimal.

Chapter 7

Retail Jobs

Buyer

A buyer may work for a corporate buying office; a chain or individual store. Courses in garment technology and business studies are both helpful although some stores run in-house training schemes. Buyers attend fashion house previews or may work directly with a factory in the UK or abroad. One of the perks of a senior buyer is the trips overseas. A job with a large department store or group is more challenging than one in a small shop, where it may only become a case of re-ordering lines. A boutique owner, of course, is likely to be his or her own buyer. This is also where an eye for design, but not necessarily a degree, is more than useful.

Case Study

David's main love was the theatre. After school, he took a one-year art foundation course in theatre design before moving into the area of choreography. An eye for line and style, plus keen business acumen led him from selling old lace as a hobby, on behalf of someone else, to buying it and selling it in his own boutique.

> It was at the time when old lace was a fashion trend amongst the young so I could see an instant market for it. Although I can't make clothes myself, I know what will sell, so I employed people to make up wedding-dresses exclusive to my boutique, which brought me a great deal of success.

Today, David's fashionable designs no longer rely only on old lace (which he still purchases from auctions here and abroad), and his store has a well-known London name.

Stylist

A stylist is often used by fashion magazines to accessorise an outfit for a photograph. In a store, this position is liable to be called 'fashion coordinator' or 'merchandise manager'. General art and design courses are suitable for this kind of work but the turnover is very slow, and there are far fewer positions than eager applicants. The same is true of opportunities to work as a window-dresser, especially for a major department store.

Case Study

Kate took a one-year foundation course in art and design after leaving school, but as she says:

> I decided I wasn't good enough to go on in the face of the competition. I liked fashion but didn't know where to go for a job. As I'd done typing at school, I got a job in the fashion department of a monthly women's magazine as a secretary. There's always a deadline panic so I often had to run around town, picking up accessories. When I proved I was good at picking them out myself, they gave me more freedom. I took an evening-class course in photography and was eventually made assistant fashion editor.

Kate showed her strength was in styling rather than in writing, went freelance, and is now called in to supervise fashion settings for magazines, advertising and PR agencies.

Sales

The sales area of fashion is a wide one. It encompasses both the garment salesman who goes out on the road to sell for the manufacturer and the salesgirl on the fashion floor of a large department store. It may also lead to bigger and better things. Selling is a case of explaining what the product is, what it can do for the customer and how it compares with alternatives.

A job in sales may eventually lead to a sales management position where you are responsible for a team. This demands leadership since it is up to you to convince your team that your ideas and methods are the right ones. At a national sales manager level, selling and marketing are often one and the same since the manager is concerned with where and how a sales force is best deployed, what methods should be used and what incentives given, along with projected results. Further promotions might be to sales or marketing director.

Many stores have in-house training programmes for management that involve sales, marketing and buying. A school-leaver who starts off as a sales assistant may apply to join such a training scheme probably at the supervisory level; a university graduate would apply directly to be taken on as a junior management trainee.

Marketing

Basically, marketing provides a link between the manufacturer and the retailer/customer. It involves research and analysis of general fashion trends and of the market competition. It involves product planning to make sure that the garments produced meet a demand and continue to do so, and it involves sales forecasts, advertising, public relations and promotion. A marketing director will oversee all these functions in a large operation, with people working under him in speciality areas. In a small company, a marketing manager or director will deal with these functions personally.

Large companies and advertising agencies offer their own management trainee schemes and sometimes schemes specifically geared to marketing, but competition for traineeships is fierce.

The Communication, Advertising and Marketing Education Foundation Ltd (CAM) runs the best courses for marketing. It is an educational charity formed by the educational sections of the Advertising Association, the Institute of Practitioners in Advertising, and the Institute of Public Relations. Students may obtain CAM certificates and diplomas. They may choose how many certificate subjects to study for at one time, but usually complete the course by taking three a year over a two-year period. Tuition is available on full-time courses, evening classes, or correspondence courses. Full details of the scheme can be obtained from Abford House, 15 Wilton Road, London SW1; 01-828 7506.

The Institute of Marketing courses include a two-year part-time certificate course with exams in June and sometimes in November. Those who pass may then go on to take a one-year part-time diploma course. Details are available from Moor Hall, Cookham, Maidenhead, Berskhire; 06285 24922.

Journalism

The Newspaper Society, which gives training advice to would-be journalists, have stated that more and more entrants have university degrees, but this is not compulsory. How do you obtain a place on the journalism training scheme? As a school-leaver you may apply directly to the editor of a regional or local newspaper for employment as an in lentured trainee. If you are successful, you will serve a probationary period of six months followed by an indenture period of three years (two-and-a-half if you have two or more A levels).

You will need five O levels, four O levels and one A level, or two O levels and two A levels. In all cases, passes must include English. After the probationary period, you'll attend two eight-week block-release courses at a college accredited by the National Council for the Training of Journalists — one during the first year of indenture and one in the second. In most cases a period of two-and-a-half years must have elapsed before you can take the proficiency test.

Names and addresses of regional and local newspapers can be found in Benn's *UK Press Directory* or Willing's *Press Guide.* Copies are available in local reference libraries.

Another way is to apply to the National Council for the Training of Journalists (NCTJ) for a place on the one-year full-time pre-entry course. Their address is Carlton House, Hemnall Street, Epping, Essex. Full-time one-year courses in newspaper journalism are held at the following colleges:

Darlington College of Technology, Cleveland Avenue,
   Darlington, County Durham DL3 7BB
Harlow Technical College, College Gate, The High, Harlow,
   Essex CM20 1LT
Highbury College of Technology, Dovercourt Road,
   Cosham, Portsmouth PO6 2SA
Preston Polytechnic, Corporation Street, Preston PR1 2TQ
Richmond College of Further Education, Spinkhill Drive,
   Sheffield S13 8FD
South Glamorgan Institute of Higher Education, Colchester
   Avenue, Cardiff CF3 7XR.

To qualify, you need at least two O levels and two A levels
which include English. Apply to the NCTJ enclosing a
stamped addressed envelope. If you are found suitable, you
will take a written test and then, if successful, you will
attend a selection interview. At the time of writing, college
fees can be as much as £600. After the course, trainees are
indentured for two years after a three-month probationary
period. One-and-a-half years of practical experience are
necessary before taking the proficiency test.

Some newspaper groups have their own in-house training
schemes which meet the NCTJ requirements. These are:
The Croydon Advertiser Group; East Midland Allied Press;
Thomson Regional Newspapers; Express and Star, Wolverhampton; Westminster Press Ltd; Kent and Sussex Courier;
Eastern Counties Newspapers Ltd; and United Newspapers Ltd.

Graduates apply in the same way as school-leavers.
One-year postgraduate diploma courses in journalism are
available at University College, 34 Cathedral Road, Cardiff
CF1 9YG, and at The City University, St John Street,
London EC1. After completing this course successfully
and joining a provincial newspaper, you will be indentured
for one year and nine months including a three-month
period of probation. The proficiency test may be taken
after one year.

Fashion Writer

These days, it is recommended to complete a journalism

course or work on a National Council of Journalism course scheme operated in conjunction with regional and provincial papers. Many publications will only accept NUJ members as staff, and you can't be an NUJ member until you have passed the requisite exams.

The ability to write (as opposed to reporting, which can be taught), however, comes naturally. You can certainly still get in via the back door if you're willing to type, make the coffee, and do whatever else needs to be done.

Specialised writing courses are available (fashion, for example), but they won't necessarily gain you the employment of your choice. Taking a course in tourism does not ensure a job as a travel writer and neither will a fashion writing course send you to the top of the tree as fashion editor of a national. Providing you can string some words together, other knowledge of the fashion industry, say photography, or design, may help just as much.

Case Studies

Leslie is now the assistant fashion editor on Britain's top selling women's weekly magazine, but she started out wanting to be a designer. After a one-year art foundation course, she took a four-year sandwich honours degree course at a polytechnic specialising in fashion and textiles.

> There really was a speciality — I chose knitwear. Originally, I'd thought to study textiles only, but I finally opted for a course that offered a bit of both. A sandwich course was good for me because it gave me industrial knowledge. Block-release allowed me to actually work at manufacturing concerns.
>
> My main aim was to work with ideas and predictions and, after finishing my course, I freelanced for a while doing just that — supplementing a very minimal income by working at British Home Stores. Then I spent three years with a small company where I wrote monthly fashion reports that more or less translated couturier fashion into street fashion. My present job involves frequent meetings about themes for subsequent issues; attending press previews and helping pick out what fashions we will photograph. I organise the accessories and supervise photo sessions as well as write copy for the feature and captions.

Angela was the assistant editor's secretary of a large women's magazine, but she was ambitious. When a vacancy arose for a similar job in the fashion department, she applied. She was in the right place at the right time; knew how the magazine worked and who did what; learned the basics of production and was recommended for being bright by her immediate boss.

> Although you might say it was side-stepping from one secretarial post to another, I knew that departments are very undermanned. Sooner or later the fashion editor would ask if someone could help out — picking up clothes, dropping them, writing a paragraph or setting up a photo session. If you prove you can do what is asked of you, you are noticed — and given more to do. It may be a longer route to a fashion writer's job, but it can work.

Fashion Copywriter

To be a copywriter, you might opt to take a journalism course after school, although a copywriting course *per se* would be preferable if you can find one. Copywriters don't need to be imaginative writers. Indeed, they don't have the space to play with purple prose and must be economic with their words. Whether or not copywriters work for a mail order catalogue, a tour operator or an advertising agency, they will undoubtedly be writing about the same thing time and time again. They must therefore have the ability to say the same thing in different ways without being bored or boring.

Case Study

Sarah is a copywriter with an advertising agency.

> I knew what I wanted to do when I left school so I took a one-year's copywriting course at Watford College — that's about the only one with a specific kind of course. We were given imaginary briefs and had to put together a portfolio which was assessed at the end of the course. It's a diploma course that includes four weeks of actual work in an agency of your choice.
>
> I was lucky because I won a scholarship to join McCann's with guaranteed paid work for a year and the possibility of

staying on afterwards if they liked my work. They call it the Peter Hodgeson Scheme and they take the top student from the Watford course once a year. As a copywriter here I work closely with the art director. The account director gives us a brief on. the product — tells us the target market and what the client's problems are. Then we discuss how best to put their message across. A junior copywriter can earn between £5,000 and £6,000 per annum; a senior copywriter, more, and eventually someone can move up to creative director.

Fashion Photographer

The fashion photographer may opt for relevant training or may trust to luck and determination. Courses recognised by the British Institute of Professional Photography include technical and creative aspects of professional photography. An alternative might be a City and Guilds qualification in general photography. Degree courses are available in the subject and, in addition, some art and design courses include photography as an option.

New college-leavers may find jobs as photographic assistants — in a studio, or for a freelance established photographer. They might decide to set themselves up as freelancers themselves, which will mean knocking on a multitude of doors belonging to art directors of publi-cations and advertising agencies, in order to show them portfolios.

A press photographer must be adaptable enough to shoot a number of situations, people and products — not only fashion. Press photographers often start work with regional and provincial newspapers through an apprentice-ship scheme run by the National Council for the Training of Journalists.

School-leavers with an interest in photography, or an instinctive knack with a camera, may be lucky enough to obtain some type of assistant work in a studio where, if they are keen enough, they will learn all they need to know to work on their own.

Case Studies

Up-and-coming fashion photographer, *James*, left school

not knowing what he wanted to do, ended up qualifying as a civil engineer and only took up photography in 1980.

My girlfriend was a model and when I saw her test shots and what she was paying, I thought I could do as well. With one camera and one lens, I simply practised on her, taking location shots during the summers of 1978 and 1979. I made some botches, and some hits and when Valerie Askew saw some of my pictures in my girlfriend's book, she sent along other models for test sessions. I lost more money than I earned but as chance would have it, I met a photographer at a party who had space in his studio. The assistants there taught me about studio work and I got my first proper paid-for and booked magazine assignment in 1981. Even by the end of that year I had to work in a restaurant to help support myself, but gradually more and more people rang me up for work.

I took on my own studio and assistant in October 1983 and haven't looked back. I do a lot of location stuff around England and have sold a bunch of shots on spec — possibly because my brother and his girlfriend are both models! The work is as varied as it can be — only the other day, I was on session with Miss World. And now, too, I've cracked the advertising side.

My regret is that I never was a true assistant during my career, but a course on photography doesn't necessarily give you the experience — only the technical knowhow — and even though something like lighting can be tricky, it's not impossible. My own assistant is a school-leaver who went on a one-day-a-week course under a Youth Training Scheme.

Robert dropped out of school after only one year of A levels, but decided to take up photography.

Dad owned a camera shop so I was one step ahead of the game in that I knew all about cameras and how to load and change lenses. I simply knocked on doors until I was given as assistant's job in a group of photographers' studios. I first worked in still life and then moved to fashion as an assistant. Now I'm freelancing.

I think if someone knows the basics of photography, they don't need a course, but they should be able to handle people. When I got my first assistant's job, all I had with me were some holiday snaps yet I was chosen over people with a degree in photography. In my present position, I set up lights, backgrounds, organise and test models. Some photographers allow you to use their studio and equipment, which is a big plus factor. Others don't and then you must collect your own equipment, an expensive prospect. As an assistant, you may only earn £30 or so a week, maybe as much as £60, but a top photographer could have a turnover of £80,000 per annum.

Illustrator

The area of illustration is a very broad one. It may mean graphic design with typography and lettering, 3-D design, or even pure design with the emphasis on drawing. It is wise to take an all-round course that allows you to specialise during the second and third years though there are some courses that specialise throughout. Courses are available at degree, vocational and foundation levels and are likely to be geared to project-based work with briefs and deadlines. The psychology of how to deal with clients, how to present work and respond to briefs, is all covered in graphic design courses.

Job prospects in fashion illustration include full-time work or freelance opportunities with a magazine or advertising agency. Art directors are potential employers and the Association of Illustrators is a professional body worth contacting, as it provides advice and promotion.

If you can freelance whilst still at college, so much the better, and the degree or diploma show at the end of a course often brings in art directors seeking new talent. If you're prepared to pay out 25 per cent and more of any commission you might receive, an artist's agent may be a valuable aide. For a list of agents, contact the Association of Illustrators, 17 Carlton House Terrace, London SW1.

Graphic design courses that include illustration may well lead to full-time employment as junior art director, leading to senior positions with salaries of around £60,000 per annum.

Case Study

Chris is in his first job — a junior art director with an advertising agency.

After school, I took a one-year foundation course at Hornsey College of Art covering general areas and specialising in

3-D design. The last three months you actually work in an agency. After that course, I took a three-year BA degree course at Kingston Polytechnic concentrating on 3-D design which included exhibition, theatre and TV set-work. After I finished, I did the rounds of the agencies with a portfolio. I made up imaginary briefs on imaginary products and followed through with how I thought they should be presented.

My present job means being one of a team. Once you're given a brief, you work out with the copywriter how to solve the problem with creative flair. You've got to communicate in a compelling way when you've identified the product and the message. 3-D design is particularly necessary for TV which forms 60 per cent of the business at the agency where I work. A junior like myself is likely to earn £4,500 to £6,000 per annum.

Advertising Agencies

Although the creative department (copywriters, art directors etc) is an important one in an advertising agency, there is another essential division — account management — which covers the work done for one product/client. An account executive (whose superior is an account director) has the routine contact with the client and supervises work on that particular account. The account management section is the one which the client shouts at when he doesn't like the creative results, whilst the creative staff might also blame management if their ideas are not properly represented to the client.

The way to an account management job, as indeed to any fashion merchandising or marketing position, may well be a course that includes marketing and business studies, but more general degree courses can also prepare you for this type of work as shown by the following case study.

Case Study

David graduated from Bristol University with a BA in history and spent the following year as a research assistant at the House of Commons before moving to an advertising agency as a trainee account executive.

An arts degree is good for this job because it forces you to be organised and to synthesise information taken from a vast number of sources. This way of thinking is as relevant in advertising as it was in history, for here you often have to make an instant decision based on a variety of information. Account management is sort of being master of all trades. An account man is the link between the client and the agency. He must understand the client's needs and represent them to the creative department – and vice versa, so that everyone works in harmony. The account man also has to help the client develop new products and ideas and launch them. An executive's salary is around £5,000 to £6,500 and the account director's up to £16,000 per annum.

Public Relations Officer

The fashion PRO may work for a manufacturer, a store, or a consultancy handling several accounts. The range of skills required may be highly varied and include knowledge of photography, design, print work and layout if the job involves production of brochures and display material. Some writing ability is necessary to put together press releases that will appeal to the media, and an organisational talent is also needed for press shows, promotions, special events and possibly trade fairs.

The PRO is a communicator between the client and the media, and sometimes the public. He or she must become thoroughly acquainted with the product and be able to show its strong points to the relevant people. The ability to get along with people is essential, and so is fluent speech since the PRO will have to explain policies, plans and achievements and convince people. Creativity is another requirement and being able to work under pressure, a must.

Any communications or marketing course from diploma to degree levels will teach about the various areas of public relations and the Institute of Public Relations has its own exams. A degree in marketing, communications or business studies may lead eventually to a highly paid managerial job, but it should be pointed out that one can also enter public relations via the secretarial route.

Case Study

Vanessa is only 20 but she is chief assistant to the owner of a fashion-orientated PR consultancy. After leaving school with some O levels, she took a one-year secretarial and business studies course plus A level English, and followed this with a year's art foundation course, specialising in graphics and photography.

> Getting into PR because you want to be a PR is a bit of a Catch 22 situation. If you apply for a specific position, you're asked what practical experience you have. Of course, until you're given that first job, you don't have any practical experience, however many courses you may have taken.
>
> What I did was to be persistent, writing loads of letters to as many fashion houses and agencies as I could, 'selling' myself. This led to taking a short-term unpaid position helping out typing, picking up clothes etc. Although this may seem a bit lowly, if you have the sparkle, it will be recognised. I joined this consultancy as a junior and now work with about 15 fashion clients. My job involves creating stories, recognising what will make a good story, organising events and press shows, liaising on a day-to-day basis with the fashion press, and writing releases. I feel that 'sparkle' is more important than academic achievements, at least for this branch of the industry.

Fashion Model

There are no specific academic qualifications for becoming a top photographic model although some O levels (or equivalent) are recommended. You must, however, be 5ft 7ins or 5ft 8ins tall and have a hip size of no more than 35ins. (Models who are 5ft 6ins or 5ft 11ins would have to be very special for an agency to risk taking them on.) Agencies point out that work experience of about a year after school may be useful — to prepare yourself for handling people and the business world. An expensive 'modelling school course' is not a necessity, although it may help deportment and personality development.

The majority of top modelling agencies are in London, where most of the work is. School-leavers considering this type of fashion career are advised to make an appointment to see one of the agencies approved by the

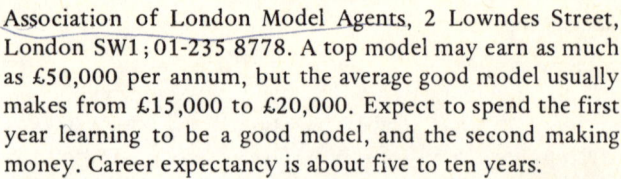

Association of London Model Agents, 2 Lowndes Street, London SW1; 01-235 8778. A top model may earn as much as £50,000 per annum, but the average good model usually makes from £15,000 to £20,000. Expect to spend the first year learning to be a good model, and the second making money. Career expectancy is about five to ten years.

Would-be models should at least bring snapshots of themselves when they visit an agency, and a good agent should be able to tell at a glance whether you have potential. The agent may well tell you to do something with your hair, have a tooth capped or lose weight, but if interested, will arrange a test reel with a photographer. This should cost you in the region of £15 to £20.

For the initial few months, you will be spending money on photo tests, hairdos and make-up whilst you learn how to relax in front of the camera, and how to cope with your looks. Expect the test period to cost around £200. You will be advised of a list of basic accessories which you should always have with you and be put on the 'test board'. It may take up to six months for your first paid job but you will be paid the full hourly rate — there is no 'new girl/boy' rate. (Training is very similar for would-be male models, but obviously with less emphasis on make-up.) At first, you may only work one day a week but this should gradually increase if you are willing to learn and be disciplined. (Working only one day a week, a model may still earn more than a secretary.)

An agency generally takes 20 to 25 per cent of a model's earnings as its fee. There are two methods of payment: for 20 per cent the model must wait for the client to pay the agency the fee; for 25 per cent the model receives 60 per cent of earnings ten days after invoicing the agency and the remaining 15 per cent after the client has settled the bill.

Models are required for editorial publications, TV commercials, advertising, catalogues, fashion shows and wholesale houses. Only the fashion-show (or catwalk) model needs to be 5ft 9ins or more. Wholesale houses tend to be less strict as regards height and measurement requirements. Not all agencies deal with that area. Those who do include Whittaker, Gavin Robinson, Count 8, Myrtle Winstone and Julia Hunt. Remember, there are only two seasons in warehousing modelling so you couldn't make a career from that alone.

Case Study

Catherine has been a model for two years with Askews and is currently one of the best.

> Valerie Askew sees new girls every Friday but only takes on four at a time to groom and develop. The difference between my first test shots and the pictures now in my portfolio is incredible! Only through constantly being photographed and analysing the results can you develop an individual style and, with it, confidence. I am far more adventurous now with dress than I used to be.
>
> Models have to be adaptable and that means keeping a reasonably simple hairstyle, washing it every day, and being able to handle it. I was introduced to a top hair stylist right at the beginning, who took me on free. This often does happen when the hairdresser likes you. It's good for their publicity and a perk for you. The same thing happened with one of my test photographers — an assistant — who gave me free pictures in return for my time, since we both needed the practice.
>
> The perks of the job include meeting lots of interesting people, going to fancy places, travelling abroad and being surrounded by an aura of glamour. But it is also hard work. When the product being sold is you, you have to look after it and that means exercise, healthy eating and early nights. A spot or cold sore could lose you a £300-a-day assignment. Although you have to stay underweight because the camera adds pounds, you must have stamina to, say, wear fur coats under hot lights or be photographed on a beach when it's freezing cold.

Part 2

Chapter 8

Courses Available

Keys to codes for entry level to courses

N	None. A good level of education is expected but there are no specific requirements
O	O levels, usually more than one, and often particular subjects are required
A	A levels required
D	Postgraduate course: first degree or equivalent qualifications required
P	Professional course for which a previous professional qualification or (in some cases) relevant work experience is required
A/O	CNAA courses which can be entered either with A levels or O levels via a foundation course

Abbreviations used for colleges, polytechnics, etc.

AA	Academy of Art
Ag & TC	Agricultural and Technical College
BC	Borough College
C	College
CA & AdStd	College of Art and Adult Studies
CA & D	College of Art and Design
CA & T	College of Art and Technology
CAT	College of Advanced Technology
CB & P	College of Building and Printing
CComm	College of Commerce
CCT	College of Commerce and Technology
CD	College of Design
CEd	College of Education

CFE	College of Further Education
CHE	College of Higher Education
CT	College of Technology
FEC	Further Education College
HEC	Higher Education College
I	Institute
IHE	Institute of Higher Education
MetC	Metropolitan College
MetIHE	Metropolitan Institute of Higher Education
Poly	Polytechnic
SA	School of Art
SA & C	School of Art and Crafts
SA & D	School of Art and Design
SAcc	School of Accountancy
SchIns	School of Insurance
T & AC	Technology and Art College
TC	Technical College

Fashion, Textile Design and Embroidery

CNAA Courses

Glasgow SA. Full-time. *BA/BA(Hons) in design (embroidered and woven textiles).* A/O

Glasgow SA. Full-time. *BA/BA(Hons) in design (printed textiles).* A/O

Kidderminster CFE, Wolverhampton Poly. Sandwich. *BA(Hons) in design of carpets and related textiles.* A/O

Harrow CHE, Kingston Poly, Bristol Poly. Full-time. *BA(Hons) in fashion.* A/O

St Martin's SA, Newcastle Poly. Sandwich. *BA(Hons) in fashion.* A/O

North East London Poly. Sandwich. *BA in fashion (design with marketing).* A/O

Brighton Poly. Sandwich. *BA(Hons) in fashion textiles design and administration.* A/O

Trent Poly. Sandwich. *BA(Hons) in knitwear design.* A/O

Huddersfield Poly. Sandwich. *BSc(Hons) in textile design.* A/O

Leicester Poly. Full-time. *BA(Hons) in textiles fashion (contour design)*. A/O

Loughborough CA & D, Goldsmiths' C, Manchester Poly, Birmingham Poly, Ulster Poly. Full-time. *BA(Hons) in textiles fashion (embroidery)*. A/O

Leicester Poly, Trent Poly, Middlesex Poly, Ravensbourne CA & D, St Martin's SA, Liverpool Poly, Manchester Poly, Gloucestershire CAT, Birmingham Poly. Full-time. *BA(Hons) in textiles/fashion (fashion)*. A/O

Preston Poly. Sandwich. *BA(Hons) in textiles/fashion (fashion)*. A/O

Leicester Poly. Full-time. *BA(Hons) in textiles/fashion (footwear design)*. A/O

Trent Poly, Central SA & D. Full-time. *BA(Hons) in textiles/fashion (textile design)*. A/O

Leicester Poly, Loughborough CA & D, West Surrey CA & D, Camberwell SA & C, Liverpool Poly, Manchester Poly, Winchester SA, Birmingham Poly, Ulster Poly. Full-time. *BA(Hons) in textiles/fashion (woven and printed textiles)*. A/O

Middlesex Poly. Full-time. *BA(Hons) in textiles/fashion (printed textiles)*. A/O

Middlesex Poly. Full-time. *BA(Hons) in textiles/fashion (woven textiles)*. A/O

Duncan of Jordanstone CA (Dundee). Full-time. *BA(Hons) in decorative design (woven textiles)*. A/O

Duncan of Jordanstone CA (Dundee). Full-time. *BA(Hons) in decorative design (printed textiles)*. A/O

Certificate and Diploma Courses

Chesterfield CA & D, Derby Lonsdale CHE, Southend CT, Canterbury CA, Eastbourne CFE, Epsom SA & D, Medway CD, Reigate SA & D, Croydon C, Cleveland CA & D, Salford CT, Wigan CT, Berkshire CA & D, Southampton CHE, West Sussex CD, Bournemouth and Poole CA & D, Bristol Poly, Plymouth CA & D, Dewsbury and Batley T & AC, Doncaster MetIHE, Granville C (Sheffield), York CA & T, Gwent CHE.

Full-time. *Society of Industrial Artists and Designers: diploma membership (fashion textiles).* O

Somerset CA & T. Full-time. *DATEC: higher national diploma of business studies, design of textiles and surface pattern specialism.* AP

Salford CT. Full-time. *BTEC: higher national diploma in business studies, fashion design specialism.* AP

Somerset CA & T, Herefordshire CA & D. Full-time. *DATEC: certificate in design for clothing manufacture.* NO

Waltham Forest C, Tameside CT, Bournville SA & C, Leek CFE & SA, Scarborough TC, North East Wales IHE. Full-time. *DATEC: certificate in fashion.* NO

Wigan CT, Southampton CHE. Day-release. *DATEC: certificate in fashion.* NO

Cleveland CA & D. Full-time. *DATEC: certificate in fashion (light clothing).* NO

Barnfield C (Luton), Great Yarmouth CA & D, Chesterfield CA & D, Derby Lonsdale CHE, Loughborough CA & D, West Nottinghamshire CFE, Southend CT, Epsom SA & D, Hastings CAT, Medway CD, Croydon C, Hounslow BC, London C Fashion, Newcastle CA & T, Wigan CT, Berkshire CA & D, Southampton CHE, West Sussex CD, Bournemouth and Poole CA & D, Plymouth CA & D, Salisbury CA, Coventry TC, Mid-Warwickshire CFE, Stafford CFE, Stoke Cauldon CFE, Bradford and Ilkley Community C, Doncaster MetIHE, Granville C (Sheffield), Jacob Kramer C (Leeds), York CA & T, Gwent CHE. Full-time. *DATEC: diploma in fashion.* NO

Gloucestershire CAT. Day-release. *DATEC: diploma in fashion.* NO

South Fields CFE (Leicester). Full-time. *DATEC: diploma in fashion (knitwear).* NO

Jacob Kramer C (Leeds). Full-time. *DATEC: diploma in surface pattern design.* NO

Great Yarmouth CA & D, Derby Lonsdale CHE, Blackburn CT & D, West Sussex CD, Bradford and Ilkley Community C. Full-time. *DATEC: diploma in textile design.* NO

Canterbury CA. Full-time. *DATEC: diploma in fashion and textiles.* NO

Stafford CFE, York CA & T. Full-time. *DATEC: higher certificate in fashion.* AP

Derby Lonsdale CHE, Loughborough CA & D, Epsom SA & D, Medway CD, London C Fashion, Cleveland CA & D, Berkshire CA & D, Bournemouth and Poole CA & D. Full-time. *DATEC: higher diploma in fashion.* AP

Derby Lonsdale CHE, Chelsea SA, Cleveland CA & D, Huddersfield Poly. Full-time. *DATEC: higher diploma in textile design.* AP

Blackburn CT & D. Day-release. *DATEC: higher diploma in textile design.* AP

Bishop Auckland TC. Day-release. *Regional Award: certificate in fashion and clothing design.* Also evenings

Dewsbury and Batley T & AC. Full-time. *Regional Award: certificate in fashion design.*

Barnsley School of Art. Full-time. *Regional Award: certificate in surface pattern design.*

Dewsbury and Batley T & AC. Full-time. *Regional Award: certificate in textile design.*

Burnley CA & T, Oldham CT, Southport CAD. Full-time. *Regional Award: 758 Manufacturing and Retail Fashion (certificate in art and design)*

Rochdale CA, Southport CA & D, Stockport CT. Full-time. *Regional Award: 758 Textile and Pattern Design (certificate in art and design).* Day-release at Walsall CA

Monkwearmouth CFE. Full-time. *Regional Award: diploma in applied design (textile fashion)*

West Surrey CA & D. Full-time. *Regional Award: diploma in art and design (textile design)*

Reigate SA & D, Cleveland CA & D. Full-time. *Regional Award: higher diploma in art and design (textile design)*

West Surrey CA & D. Full-time. *Regional Award: diploma in art and design (woven textiles)*

Berkshire CA & D, Southampton CHE. Full-time. *Regional Award: higher diploma in design (fashion)*

Southend CT. Full-time. *Regional Award: diploma in design (textile design)*

Southampton CHE, Plymouth CA & D. Full-time. *Regional Award: diploma in fashion*

Merton TC. Full-time. *College Award: design technician certificate (fashion).* N

London C Fashion. Day-release and full-time. *College Award: certificate in embroidery.* O

Nene C (Northampton). Full-time. *College Award: certificate in fashion*

Eastbourne CFE. Full-time. *College Award: certificate in fashion design*

London C Fashion. Full-time. *College Award: certificate in fashion modelling.* O

Loughborough CA & D. Sandwich. *College Award: certificate in the teaching of dress and embroidery*

Sheffield City Poly. Day-release and evenings. *College Award: certificate in textile arts and fashion.* N

Eastbourne CFE. Full-time. *College Award: certificate in textiles (printed)*

Eastbourne CFE. Full-time. *College Award: certificate in textiles (woven)*

Salford CT. Full-time. *College Award: advanced certificate in fashion design.* N

South Gwent CFE. Evenings. *College Award: pre-CGLI certificate in fashion*

Brighton Poly. Day-release. *College Award: diploma in creative embroidery.* O

Redbridge TC. Full-time. *College Award: diploma in dress and light clothing*

Amersham CFEA & D, Weston-super-Mare TC & SA, Coventry TC, East Warwickshire CFE, Stafford CFE, Ulster Poly. Full-time. *College Award: diploma in fashion.* OA

Chesterfield CA & D, Dyfed CA. Full-time. *College Award: diploma in fashion design*

Gloucestershire CAT. Day-release. *College Award: diploma in fashion technology*

Huddersfield Poly. Full-time. *College Award: diploma in printed and woven textiles.* O

West Sussex CD. Full-time. *College Award: advanced diploma in printed textiles*

Amersham CFEA & D, Croydon C. Full-time. *College Award: diploma in textile design*

Dewsbury and Batley T & AC. Full-time. *College Award: diploma in textiles and printed surfaces*

Dyfed CA. Full-time. *College Award: diploma in woven textile design*

West Sussex CD. Full-time. *College Award: advanced diploma in fashion design*

Salford CT. Full-time. *College Based: advanced diploma in fashion design.* N

Southampton CHE. Day-release. *College Based: advanced creative embroidery.* N

Clothing Manufacture and Tailoring

CNAA Course

Manchester Poly. Sandwich. *BA in clothing studies.* A

Certificate and Diploma Courses

Belfast CT. Full-time. *Clothing and Footwear Institute: associate, Part I and II.* A and P. Sandwich for both parts at Teesside Poly, Scottish C Textiles (Galashiels)

Kilburn Poly, London C Fashion, Southgate TC, Handsworth TC, Pontypridd TC. Full-time. *BTEC: certificate in clothing (C7).* NO. Block at London College of Fashion. Day-release at Southgate TC, Mabel Fletcher TC (Liverpool), Manchester Poly, Handsworth TC, Leek CFE & SA, Jacob Kramer C (Leeds), Belfast CT

London C Fashion. Block. *BTEC: certificate in clothing machine technology.* NO

Medway CD, London C Fashion, Southgate TC, Manchester Poly, Oxford CFE, Handsworth TC, Jacob Kramer C (Leeds), Belfast CT. Full-time. *BTEC: diploma in clothing (C7).* NO

London C Fashion. Full-time. *BTEC: higher certificate in clothing (C7)*. AP. Day-release at London C Fashion, Belfast CT. Evenings at Handsworth TC

Medway CD, London C Fashion, Manchester Poly, Jacob Kramer C (Leeds). Full-time. *BTEC: higher diploma in clothing (C7)*. AP

Cardonald C (Glasgow). Day-release. *SCOTEC: certificate in clothing*. O

Henderson TC (Hawick), Lerwick FEC. Full-time. *SCOTEC: certificate in knitting techniques*. N

Cardonald C (Glasgow). Full-time and day-release. *SCOTEC: higher certificate in clothing*. AP

Cardonald C (Glasgow). Full-time. *Training Services Division: TOPS course in clothing production*. N

Lerwick FEC, Lews Castle C (Stornoway). Full-time. *Training Services Division: TOPS course in machine knitting*. N

Rockingham CFE, Cardonald C (Glasgow). Full-time. *Training Services Division: TOPS course in sewing machinists*. N

Redbridge TC, Handsworth TC. Full-time. *CGLI 450 clothing cutters/trimmers*. N. Day-release at Handsworth TC, Cardonald C (Glasgow). Evenings. at Wigan CT, Handsworth TC

Barnfield C (Luton), Clarendon CFE (Nottingham), South Fields CFE, Colchester I, Southgate TC, Handsworth TC, Cardonald C (Glasgow). Full-time. *CGLI 460 clothing craft*. N. Day-release at Southgate TC, Tameside CT, Cannock Chase TC, Leek CFE & SA, Jacob Kramer C (Leeds), Cardonald C (Glasgow). Evenings at Southgate TC, Cannock Chase TC.

Handsworth TC. Full-time. *CGLI 460 clothing craft: wholesale, cutting and making*. Day-release at London C Fashion, Belfast CT. Evenings at London C Fashion

London C Fashion. Day-release and evenings. *CGLI 460 clothing craft: retail bespoke, cutting, tailoring*. N

Chesterfield CA & D, Mabel Fletcher TC (Liverpool), Handsworth TC, Cardonald C (Glasgow). Full-time. *CGLI 465 tailoring: craft, men's.* N. Day-release at Chesterfield CA & D, Tresham C (Kettering and Corby), Gateshead TC, Mabel Fletcher TC (Liverpool), Oxford CFE, Handsworth TC, Belfast CT, Cardonald C (Glasgow). Evenings at Chesterfield CA & D, Tresham C, South Cheshire C, Oxford CFE

Barnfield C (Luton), Cricklade C (Andover), Cardonald C (Glasgow). Full-time. *CGLI 465 tailoring: craft, women's.* N. Day-release at Barnfield C (Luton), Oxford CFE, Shrewsbury CAT, Cardonald C (Glasgow), Crosskeys CFE. Evenings at Barnfield C (Luton), Oxford CFE, Crosskeys CFE

Handsworth TC, Stoke Cauldon CFE, Doncaster MetIHE, North East Wales. Full-time. *CGLI 466 women's light clothing manufacture craft.* N. Day-release at Barnfield C (Luton), Dacorum C (Hemel Hempstead), Kilburn Poly, Redbridge TC, Bishop Auckland TC, Stoke Cauldon CFE, Doncaster MetIHE, Belfast CT, Limavady TC, Cardonald C (Glasgow). Evenings at Kilburn Poly, Redbridge TC, Wigan CT

Mabel Fletcher TC (Liverpool). Full-time. *CGLI 467 retail bespoke tailoring: advanced craft, men's.* P. Day-release at Tresham C (Kettering and Corby), Mabel Fletcher TC (Liverpool). Evenings at Tresham C (Kettering and Corby)

Barnfield C (Luton), Cardonald C (Glasgow). Day-release. *CGLI 467 retail bespoke tailoring: advanced craft, women's.* P. Evenings at Barnfield C (Luton)

Hinckley CFE. Full-time. *CGLI 468 knitting machine mechanics: craft.* N. Day-release at Hinckley CFE, Cardonald C (Glasgow)

Cardonald C (Glasgow). Day-release. *CGLI 468 knitting machine mechanics advanced craft.* P

Hinckley CFE, Mabel Fletcher TC (Liverpool). Full-time. *CGLI 469 clothing machine mechanics: craft.* N. Sandwich at Barmulloch C (Glasgow). Block at Hackney C, London C Fashion, Belfast CT.

Day-release at Hinckley CFE, People's CFE
(Nottingham), Hackney C, Cleveland TC, North
Tyneside CFE, Mabel Fletcher TC (Liverpool),
Manchester Poly, Bridgewater C, Handsworth TC,
Leek CFE & SA, Jacob Kramer C (Leeds), Belfast CT,
Barmulloch C (Glasgow)

Mabel Fletcher TC (Liverpool). Full-time. *CGLI 469
clothing machine mechanics: advanced craft.* P.
Block-release at London C Fashion. Day-release at
Hinckley CFE, London C Fashion, Leek CFE & SA,
Jacob Kramer C (Leeds), Belfast CT, Barmulloch C
(Glasgow)

Handsworth TC. Full-time. *CGLI 486 clothing manufacture
technicians, Part I, men's outerwear.* N. Day-release at
London C Fashion, Handsworth TC. Evenings at
London C Fashion

Cannock Chase TC. Day-release. *CGLI 486 clothing
manufacture technicians, Part I, dress and light clothing.*
N. Evenings at Cannock Chase TC

Mabel Fletcher TC (Liverpool). Full-time. *CGLI 486
clothing manufacture technicians, Part II.* P. Day-release
at London C Fashion, Mabel Fletcher TC (Liverpool),
Cardonald C (Glasgow). Evenings at London C Fashion

South East Derbyshire C, Fermanagh CFE, Limavady TC.
Full-time. *CGLI 6995 foundation course in garment
manufacture.* N

Cardonald C (Glasgow). Day-release. *Regional Award:
799 home machine knitting, Grade I.* Evenings at
Mabel Fletcher TC (Liverpool). Day-release and
evenings available for Grade II

Mabel Fletcher TC (Liverpool). Evenings. *Regional Award:
789 home machine knitting, Grade III*

London C Fashion. Full-time. *College Award: certificate in
clothing production.* O

Mabel Fletcher TC (Liverpool). Block. *College Award:
certificate in clothing technology*

Cardonald C (Glasgow). Full-time. *College Award: junior
technician's certificate in garment and fashion
technology.*

Cardonald C (Glasgow). Full-time. *College Award: sewing machinist instructor's certificate.* Block and day-release at Mabel Fletcher TC (Liverpool)

Mabel Fletcher TC (Liverpool). Block. *College Award: certificate for the supervisors in the clothing industry*

London C Fashion. Full-time. *College Award: certificate in bespoke tailoring.* N

London C Fashion. Day-release. *College Award: certificate in furriery.* N

London C Fashion. Full-time. *College Award: certificate in theatrical costume and cutting.* O

Manchester Poly. Sandwich. *College Award: diploma in clothing design and production management*

London C Fashion, Scottish C Textiles (Galashiels). Sandwich. *College Award: diploma in clothing management.* A

Mabel Fletcher TC (Liverpool). Full-time. *College Award: diploma in clothing manufacture and fashion*

London C Fashion, Mabel Fletcher TC (Liverpool). Full-time. *College Award: diploma in tailoring.* O

Leather and Footwear Manufacture

Certificate and Diploma Courses

Londonderry CT. Day-release. *Clothing and Footwear Institute: footwear examinations 1-6 ACFI.* P. Evenings at Wellingborough TC, Kendal CFE, West Cumbria C

Cordwainers TC. Full-time. *BTEC: certificate in footwear manufacture (C7).* NO. Day-release at Hinckley CFE, Wellingborough TC, Kendal CFE, West Cumbria C, Accrington and Rossendale C

Cordwainers TC. Full-time. *BTEC: diploma in footwear design.* NO

Nene C (Northampton). Full-time. *BTEC: higher diploma in leather technology (C7).* AP

Cordwainers TC. Full-time. *BTEC: higher certificate in footwear manufacture (upper department).* AP.

Day-release at South Fields CFE (Leicester), Kendal
CFE, Accrington and Rossendale C

Cordwainers TC. Full-time. *BTEC: higher certificate in
footwear manufacture (pattern cutting).* AP. Day-release
at South Fields CFE (Leicester), Kendal CFE,
Accrington and Rossendale C

Cordwainers TC. Full-time. *BTEC: higher certificate in
footwear manufacture (buttoning departments).* AP.
Day-release at South Fields CFE (Leicester), Kendal
CFE, Accrington and Rossendale C

South Fields CFE (Leicester). Day-release. *National
Examination Board in Supervisory Studies: certificate
(footwear manufacture).* N

Walsall CA. Full-time. *Training Services Division: TOPS
course in leathergoods manufacture.* N. Also for
leathergoods operatives

Hinckley CFE, South Fields CFE (Leicester), Cordwainers
TC. Full-time. *CGLI 454 footwear manufacture
operatives: Higher.* P. Day-release at Hinckley CFE,
South Fields CFE (Leicester), Wellingborough TC,
Kendal CFE, Accrington and Rossendale C,
Banbridge TC. Evenings at South Fields CFE,
Wellingborough TC

Nene C (Northampton). Block-release. *CGLI 456 leather
manufacture operatives: Certificate.* N. Day-release at
Kitson CT (Leeds)

Cordwainers TC. Full-time. *CGLI 470 leather goods
manufacture: Ordinary.* N. Day-release at Hinckley
CFE, Accrington and Rossendale C, Walsall CA

Hinckley CFE, Accrington and Rossendale C, Walsall CA.
Day-release. *CGLI 470 leather goods manufacture:
Advanced*

Nene C (Northampton). Block-release. *CGLI 488 leather
manufacture: dyeing and finishing technicians:
Supplementary Option.* P. Also Advanced Certificate

Londonderry CT. Day-release. *CGLI 489 footwear
manufacture technicians: Part II (upper departments
and buttoning departments).* P

Wellingborough TC. Full-time and day-release. *College Award: certificate in advanced footwear technology and management.* A

Cordwainers TC. Full-time. *College Award: special certificate in production management (footwear manufacture).* AP

South Fields CFE (Leicester). Full-time. *College Award: certificate in shoe manufacturing technology.* O

Cordwainers TC. Evenings. *College Award: craft certificates in footwear manufacture.* N

Cordwainers TC. Full-time. *College Award: craft certificate in leathergoods design studies.* O

Cordwainers TC. Day-release and evenings. *College Award: craft certificate in leathergoods manufacture.* O

Cordwainers TC. Full-time. *College Award: diploma in footwear design (Phase I).* O. Also Phase II. AP

Wellingborough TC, Cordwainers TC. Full-time. *College Award: diploma in footwear technology.* O

Cordwainers TC. Full-time, day-release and evening. *College Award: leathergoods manufacture: Ordinary/ Advanced.* O

Cordwainers TC. Full-time, day-release and evenings. *College Award: diploma in leathergoods design studies.* O

Cordwainers TC. Full-time. *College Award: diploma in leathergoods production.* O

Nene C (Northampton). Full-time. *College Award: diploma in leather technology*

Cordwainers TC. Full-time. *College Award: diploma in production management (footwear manufacture).* OA

Cordwainers TC. Full-time. *College Award: diploma in production management (leathergoods manufacture).* O

South Fields CFE (Leicester). Full-time. *College Award: diploma in shoe manufacturing technology.* O

Cordwainers TC. Full-time. *College Award: pre-diploma in footwear and leathergoods design and manufacture.* N

Airedale and Wharfedale CFE. Day-release. *College-Based: unified vocational preparation course in footwear and leather*

Graphic Design

CNAA Courses

Manchester Poly. Full-time. *BA(Hons) in design for communication media (graphic studies).* A/O

Glasgow SA. Full-time. *BA/BA(Hons) in design (graphic design).* A/O

Norwich SA, Leicester Poly, Brighton Poly, Canterbury CA, Maidstone CA, Camberwell SA & C, Central SA & D (London), Chelsea SA, Kingston Poly, London C Printing, Middlesex Poly, Ravensbourne CA & D, St Martin's SA, Newcastle Poly, Liverpool Poly, Bath AA, Bristol Poly, Exeter CA & D, Birmingham Poly, Coventry (Lanchester) Poly, Wolverhampton Poly, Hull CHE, Leeds Poly, Ulster Poly, Gwent CHE. Full-time. *BA(Hons) in graphic design.* A/O. Sandwich at Preston Poly

Middlesex Poly. Sandwich. *BA(Hons) in graphic design (graphic information, design, scientific illustration, technical illustration).* A/O

Harrow CHE. Full-time. *BA(Hons) in graphic information design.* A/O

Trent Poly. Full-time. *BA(Hons) in information graphics.* A/O

London C Printing. Sandwich. *BA(Hons) in media and production design.* A/O

North Staffordshire Poly. Full-time. *BA(Hons) multidisciplinary design course (graphics design options).* A/O

Duncan of Jordanstone CA (Dundee). Full-time. *BA/ BA(Hons) in visual communications (illustration).* A/O

Certificate and Diploma Courses

Barnfield C (Luton), Lowestoft CFE, Suffolk CH & FE,

Chesterfield CA & D, Derby Lonsdale CHE,
Southend CT, Canterbury CA, Eastbourne CFE,
Medway CD, Reigate SA & D, East Ham CT, Cleveland
CA & D, Cumbria CA & D, Blackpool and Fylde CF
& HE, Bolton MetC, Salford CT, Stockport CT,
Wigan CT, Berkshire CA & D, Southampton CHE,
West Sussex CD, Bournemouth and Poole CA & D,
Bristol Poly, Gloucestershire CAT, Plymouth CA & D,
Salisbury CA, Swindon C, Dewsbury and Batley T & AC,
Doncaster MetIHE, Granville C (Sheffield), Hull CHE,
York CA & T, West Glamorgan IHE. Full-time. *Society
of Industrial Artists and Designers: diploma membership
(graphics).* O

Barnfield C (Luton), Lincolnshire CA, South Fields CFE
(Leicester), Ware C, Exeter CA & D, Weston-super-Mare
TC & SA, Bournville SA & C, East Warwickshire CFE,
Solihull CT, Sutton Coldfield CFE, Percival Whitley
CFE (Halifax), Rotherham CAT, Scarborough TC.
Full-time. *DATEC: certificate in graphic design.* NO.
Day-release at Loughton CFE, Wigan CT,
Farnborough CT, Coventry TC.

Barnfield C (Luton), Farnborough CT. Day-release.
DATEC: higher certificate in graphic design. AP

Barnfield C (Luton), Great Yarmouth CA & D,
Suffolk CH & FE, Derby Lonsdale CHE, Lincolnshire
CA, Loughborough CA & D, West Nottinghamshire CFE,
Colchester I, Loughton CFE, Ware C, Canterbury CA,
Epsom SA & D, Hastings CAT, Medway CD, Croydon C,
East Ham CT, Hounslow BC, London C Printing,
Newcastle CA & T, Central Liverpool CFE, Southport
CAD, Tameside CT, Wigan CT, Berkshire CA & D,
Southampton CHE, Bournemouth and Poole CA & D,
Cornwall TC, Plymouth CA & D, Salisbury CA, South
Devon TC, Swindon C, North Warwickshire CT & A,
Bradford and Ilkley Community C, Doncaster MetIHE,
Granville C (Sheffield), Jacob Kramer C (Leeds),
Scarborough TC, Wakefield District C, York CA & T,
North East Wales IHE. Full-time. *DATEC: diploma in
graphic design.* NO. Day-release at Stourbridge CT & A

Farnborough CT. Full-time. *DATEC: diploma in graphic design with business studies.* NO

Southend CT, Wirral MC, Portsmouth CAD & FE, Gloucestershire CAT. Full-time. *DATEC: diploma in visual communications.* NO

Lincolnshire CA, Ealing CHE, Cleveland CA & D, Bolton MetC, Granville C (Sheffield), Sheffield City Poly, North East Wales IHE. Full-time. *DATEC: higher diploma in visual communication.* AP

Barnfield C (Luton), Dunstable C, Great Yarmouth CA & D, Derby Lonsdale CHE, Loughborough CA & D, Colchester I, Southend CT, Watford C, Epsom SA & D, Medway CD, Barnet C, East Ham CT, Hounslow BC, Richmond-upon-Thames C, Cleveland CA & D, Cumbria CA & D, Southampton CHE, Bournemouth and Poole CA & D, Cornwall TC, Salisbury CA, Somerset CA & T, Swindon C, Jacob Kramer C (Leeds), York CA & T. Full-time. *DATEC: higher diploma in graphic design.* AP

Aberdeen CCom, Cardonald C (Glasgow), Dundee CCom, Falkirk CT, Telford CFE (Edinburgh). Full-time. *SCOTEC: diploma in art-design.* O

Doncaster MetIHE. Full-time. *DATEC: higher diploma in advertising graphics.* AP

Newcastle CA & T. Full-time. *DATEC: higher diploma in advertising design and photography.* AP

Barnsley School of Art, Dewsbury and Batley T & AC, Percival Whitley CFE (Halifax), Rotherham CAT. Full-time. *Regional Award: certificate in advertising design.* Day-release at Dewsbury and Batley T & AC. Also evenings

Northumberland TC. Full-time. *Regional Award: certificate in commercial and industrial design*

Suffolk CH & FE. Full-time. *Regional Award: certificate in design (graphic design)*

Harrogate CA & AdStd. Full-time. *Regional Award: certificate in graphic design*

Burnley CA & T, Mabel Fletcher TC (Liverpool), Mid-Cheshire CFE, Oldham CT, Rochdale CA,

Stockport CT, Leek CFE & SA. Full-time. *Regional Award: 758 advertising design (certificate in art and design).* Day-release at Leek CFE & SA

Northumberland TC. Full-time. *Regional Award: diploma in applied design (graphics)*

York CA & T. Full-time. *Regional Award: advanced certificate in graphic design*

Reigate SA & D. Full-time. *Regional Award: higher diploma in art and design (graphic design)*

Barnfield C (Luton), Lowestoft CFE, Southend CT, Southampton CHE, Swindon C. Full-time. *Regional Award: diploma in design (graphics)*

Berkshire CA & D. Full-time. *Regional Award: higher diploma in design (graphics)*

Colchester I, Croydon C, Gloucestershire CAT, Plymouth CA & D. Full-time. *Regional Award: diploma in graphic design*

Southampton CHE. Day-release. *College Award: certificate in advertising design.* N

Herefordshire CA & D. Full-time. *College Award: certificate in design*

Nene C (Northampton), Eastbourne CFE, Coventry TC, Walsall CA. Full-time. *College Award: certificate in graphic design.* N. Day-release at Coventry TC, Rupert Stanley CFE (Belfast)

Salford CT. Full-time. *College Award: advanced certificate in graphic design*

Eastbourne CFE. Full-time. *College Award: certificate in illustration*

City and Guilds London AS. Full-time. *College Award: certificate in advanced and experimental lettering*

East Ham CT. Full-time. *College Award: certificate in studio graphics*

Solihull CT. Full-time. *College Award: higher certificate in vocational graphic design.* A

Solihull CT. Full-time. *College Award: certificate in vocational reprographic design.* O

Barking CT. Full-time. *College Award: diploma in advertising design*

Wakefield District C. Day-release and evening. *College Award: diploma in advanced graphic studies*

Huddersfield Poly. Full-time. *College Award: diploma in graphics and advertising design.* O

Watford C, City and Guilds London AS, Stockport CT. Full-time. *College Award: diploma in graphic arts*

Nene C (Northampton), Amersham CFEA & D, East Ham CT, Wimbledon SA, Blackpool and Fylde CF & HE, Weston-super-Mare TC & SA, Dewsbury and Batley T & AC, Hull CHE, West Glamorgan IHE. Full-time. *College Award: diploma in graphic design*

Lincolnshire CA, Salford CT. Full-time. *College Award: diploma in graphic design (Advanced)*

Amersham CFEA & D, Barking CT. Full-time. *College Award: diploma in illustration*

Harrow CHE. Full-time. *College Award: higher diploma in illustration*

Solihull CT. Full-time. *College Award: diploma in vocational graphic design.* O

Thurrock TC. Full-time. *College Award: diploma in visual communication*

North Warwickshire CT & A. Full-time. *College-Based: vocational graphic design course.* N

Photography

CNAA Courses

Harrow CHE. Full-time. *BA(Hons) in applied photography, film and TV.* A/O

Central London Poly. Full-time. *BA(Hons) in film and photographic arts.* A/O

Manchester Poly. Full-time. *BA(Hons) in design for communication media.* A/O

Harrow CHE. Day-release. *BA in photographic media studies.* A/O

Central London Poly. Full-time. *BSc/BSc(Hons) in photographic sciences.* A

Derby Lonsdale CHE, Trent Poly. Full-time. *BA(Hons) in photographic studies.* A/O

West Surrey CA & D. Full-time. *BA(Hons) in photography, film and video.* A/O

London C Printing. Full-time. *BA(Hons) in visual communications.* A/O

West Midlands CHE. Full-time. *BA in visual communications studies.* A/O

Diploma and Certificate Courses

Berkshire CA & D, Gloucestershire CAT, Plymouth CA & D, Napier CCT (Edinburgh). Full-time. *Institute of Incorporated Photographers: examination in vocational photography (LIIP).* O. Day-release at Richmond-upon-Thames C

Blackpool and Fylde CF & HE, Bournemouth and Poole CA & D, Salisbury CA. Full-time. *Institute of Incorporated Photographers: professional qualifying examination (AIIP).* A

Richmond CFE (Sheffield). Block. *National Council for the Training of Journalists: direct entry indentured training in press photography.* O. Also full-time *NCTJ: one-year pre-entry course in press photography.* A

Greylands International C, Brunel TC (Bristol). Full-time. *Royal Photographic Society: associateship (ARPS).* N. Evenings at North East Surrey CT

Chesterfield CA & D, Eastbourne CFE, Croydon C, Cleveland CA & D, Blackpool and Fylde CF & HE, Bournemouth and Poole CA & D, Plymouth CA & D, Salisbury CA, Dewsbury and Batley T & AC, Granville C (Sheffield), West Glamorgan IHE. Full-time. *Society of Industrial Artists and Designers: diploma membership (graphics: film and TV/photography).* O

Ware C, Wirral MC, Bournville SA & C. Full-time. *DATEC: certificate in photography.* NO

Paddington C. Day-release and evenings. *DATEC: certificate in photography.* NO. Day-release only at Richmond-upon-Thames C, Wigan CT

Barnfield C (Luton), Newcastle CA & T, Southport CAD, Tameside CT, Wigan CT, Berkshire CA & D, Plymouth CA & D, West Bromwich CCom & T,

Granville C (Sheffield), Kitson CT (Leeds). Full-time. *DATEC: diploma in photography.* NO. Day-release only at Richmond-upon-Thames C

Richmond-upon-Thames C. Day-release. *DATEC: higher certificate in professional photography*

Medway CD, Cleveland CA & D, Bournemouth and Poole CA & D, Salisbury CA. Full-time. *DATEC: higher diploma in photography.* AP

Glasgow CB & P. Day-release. *SCOTEC: certificate in photography/audio-visual technology.* N

Napier CCT (Edinburgh). Full-time. *SCOTEC: higher certificate in photography /audio-visual technology.* AP

Glasgow CB & P, Napier CCT (Edinburgh). Full-time. *SCOTEC: higher diploma in photography.* AP

Kingsway-Princeton C, Southport CAD. Full-time. *Training Services Division: TOPS course in general photography.* N

Watford C, Longland CFE (Middlesbrough). Full-time. *CGLI 6996 foundation course in multi-media communications technology.* N

Barnfield C (Luton), Medway CD, Mid-Cheshire CFE, Southport CAD, Tameside CT, Herefordshire CA & D, Stafford CFE, Dewsbury and Batley T & AC, Harrogate CA & AdStd, Glamorgan IHE. Full-time. *CGLI 744 general photography: Certificate.* N

Barnfield C (Luton), Huntingdon TC, Derby Lonsdale CHE, South Fields CFE (Leicester), Southend CT, Medway CD, North East Surrey CT, Barking CT, Newcastle CA & T, Central Liverpool CFE, Tameside CT, Gloucestershire CAT, Plymouth CA & D, Birmingham Poly, North Warwickshire CT & A, Dewsbury and Batley T & AC, Kitson CT (Leeds), Ulster Poly, North East Wales IHE, Rumney CT. Day-release. *CGLI 744 general photography: Certificate.* N

Barnfield C (Luton), Huntingdon TC, North East Surrey CT, Barking CT, Gloucestershire CAT, Herefordshire CA & D, North Warwickshire CT & A, Dewsbury and Batley T & AC, Richmond CFE (Sheffield). Evenings. *CGLI 744 general photography: certificate.* N

Plymouth CA & D, West Glamorgan IHE. Full-time.
   CGLI 744 general photography: Advanced Certificate. P
Derby Lonsdale CHE, Barking CT, Paddington C,
   Newcastle CA & T, Central Liverpool CFE,
   Plymouth CA & D, North Warwickshire CT & A,
   Kitson CT (Leeds), Ulster Poly, Glasgow CB & P,
   Napier CCT (Edinburgh). Day-release. *CGLI 744 general
   photography: Advanced Certificate.* P. Evening course at
   Barking CT, North Warwickshire CT & A
Paddington C. Day-release and evenings. *CGLI 750
   photography assistants.* Evenings only at Hounslow BC
Eastbourne CFE, Kitson CT (Leeds), Dyfed CA. Full-time.
   College Award: certificate in photography. Day-release
   at Dyfed CA
Amersham CFEA & D. Full-time. *College Award: diploma
   in advertising photography*
Barking CT, Gloucestershire CAT, Stafford CFE, West
   Glamorgan IHE. Full-time. *College Award: diploma in
   photography*
Blackpool and Fylde CF & HE. Full-time and sandwich.
   College Award: diploma in professional photography.
   Day-release at Central London Poly
Glasgow CB & P. Full-time. *College Award: diploma in
   vocational photography*
Watford C. Full-time. *College-Based: course in basic
   photography.* Day-release and evenings at Galashiels CFE
Kingsway-Princeton C. Full-time. *College-Based: course in
   vocational photography*

Journalism, Advertising and PR

CNAA Courses

Glasgow CT, Queen Margaret C (Edinburgh). Full-time.
   BA in communication studies
Sunderland Poly, Sheffield City Poly. Full-time.
   BA/BA(Hons) in communication studies. A
Trent Poly, Coventry Poly, Poly of Wales. Full-time.
   BA(Hons) in communication studies. A

Manchester Poly. Full-time. *BA(Hons) in design for communication media.* A

Ulster Poly. Full-time. *BSc(Hons) in human communication.* A

Central London Poly. Full-time. *BA(Hons) in media studies.* A

Degree Courses

Trinity and All Saints C (Leeds). Full-time. *BA/BA(Hons) (Collegiate) with public media and another subject.* A. Also *BSc/BSc(Hons)*

North Cheshire C. Full-time. University of Manchester: *BA in media and communication.* A

Dorset IHE. Full-time. University of Southampton: *BA/BA(Hons) (Collegiate) in English and media studies*

Normal CEd (Bangor). Full-time. University of Wales: *BA in communications.* A

Trinity and All Saints' C (Leeds). Full-time. *Combined subjects degree: communication arts and media option.* A

Goldsmiths' C, Bristol Poly, Normal CEd (Bangor). Full-time. *Combined subjects degree: communication studies option.* A

Certificate and Diploma Courses

Solihull CT. Full-time. *Communication Advertising and Marketing Education Foundation: certificate in communication studies.* Day-release at Distributive Trades C, Millbank CCom (Liverpool), Southampton CHE, Dorset IHE, Aberdeen CCom, Stevenson CFE (Edinburgh). Evenings at City of London Poly, Distributive Trades C, Manchester Poly, Millbank CCom (Liverpool), Bristol Poly, Matthew Boulton TC (Birmingham), Wolverhampton Poly, Aberdeen CCom, Central CCom (Glasgow)

Luton CHE, Aberdeen CCom. Day-release. *Communication Advertising and Marketing Education Foundation: advertising and marketing diploma (DipCAM).* Evenings at Luton CHE, Distributive Trades C, Wolverhampton Poly

Distributive Trades C. Evenings. *Communication Advertising and Marketing Education Foundation: public relations diploma (DipCAM)*

Luton CHE, Watford C, Distributive Trades C, Stockport CT, Bristol Poly. Full-time. *BTEC: higher national diploma in business studies, advertising specialism.* AP. Sandwich courses at Luton CHE, Stockport CT

Newcastle Poly. Full-time. *BTEC: higher national diploma in business studies design for visual communication specialism.* AP

London C Printing. Full-time. *BTEC: higher national diploma in business studies communications specialism.* AP

London C Printing. Full-time. *BTEC: higher national diploma in business studies communications specialism.* AP

Telford CFE (Edinburgh). Full-time. *SCOTBEC: SNC in media studies*

Aberdeen CCom, Bell CT (Hamilton), Dundee CCom, Falkirk CT, Kirkcaldy CT, Napier CCT (Edinburgh). Full-time. *SCOTBEC: SHND in communication studies.* P

Distributive Trades C. Day-release and evenings. *London Chamber of Commerce: advertising (Higher).* P. Also for public relations

Distributive Trades C. Day-release and evenings. *Royal Society of Arts: advertising (Stage III).* P

Chippenham TC. Full-time. *Training Services Division: TOPS course in technical authorship.* N

Norfolk CA & T, Watford C, South East London C, Highbury CT (Portsmouth), Chippenham TC, Stoke TC, Glasgow CB & P, Stevenson CFE (Edinburgh). Day-release. *CGLI 536 communication of technical information: technical communication techniques.* N. Evenings at Norfolk CA & T, Norwich City CF & HE, South East London C, CFE (Middlesbrough), Openshaw TC, Basingstoke TC, Highbury CT (Portsmouth), Stoke TC, North Lindsey CT

Norfolk CA & T, Norwich City CF & HE, Highbury CT
(Portsmouth), Chippenham TC, Glasgow CB & P. Day-
release. *CGLI 536 communication of technical
information: technical authorship.* N. Evenings at
Norfolk CA & T, South East London C, Openshaw TC,
Basingstoke TC, Highbury CT (Portsmouth)

Clarendon CFE (Nottingham), East Herts C, Eastbourne
CFE, Hastings CAT, Merton TC, Woolwich C, South
Shields MTC, Mabel Fletcher TC (Liverpool),
St Helens CT, South Cheshire C, Basingstoke TC,
Somerset CA & T, Weston-super-Mare TC & SA,
Halesowen CFE, Herefordshire TC, Fermanagh CFE,
New TC (Ballymoney), Newtownabbey TC, Cardonald C
(Glasgow), Duncraig Castle C (Plockton), Elmwood Ag
& TC (Cupar), Glasgow CFT, Springburn C (Glasgow),
South Gwent CFE. Full-time. *CGLI 732 communication
skills: Level I.* N. Block-release at Mabel Fletcher TC
(Liverpool), South Cheshire C, Gloucestershire CAT,
South Devon TC, Anniesland C (Glasgow), Cardonald C
(Glasgow), Springburn C (Glasgow). Day-release at
Peterborough TC, Hartlepool CFE, Hebburn TC,
Weaside CFE, Mabel Fletcher TC (Liverpool), South
Cheshire C, Basingstoke TC, Mid-Gloucestershire TC,
Somerset CA & T, South Devon TC, Weston-super-
Mare TC & SA, Herefordshire TC, Matthew Boulton TC
(Birmingham), Oswestry C, Airedale and Wharfedale CFE,
Granville C (Sheffield), Hull CFE, North Lindsey CT,
Ballymena TC, Fermanagh CFE, Newtownabbey TC,
Angus TC, Anniesland C (Glasgow), Cardonald C
(Glasgow), Coatbridge C, Falkirk CT, Glasgow CFT,
James Watt C (Greenock), Kirkcaldy CT, Lews
Castle C (Stornoway), Moray CFE (Elgin), Springburn C
(Glasgow). Evenings at Airedale and Wharfedale CFE,
Granville C (Sheffield).

Merton TC, Mabel Fletcher TC (Liverpool), South Cheshire
C, Basingstoke TC, Somerset CA & T, Halesowen CFE,
Fermanagh CFE, Newtownabbey TC, South Gwent CFE.
Full-time. *CGLI 732 communication skills. Level II.* P.
Block-release at Mabel Fletcher TC (Liverpool), South

Cheshire C, Gloucestershire CAT, South Devon TC.
Day-release at Peterborough TC, Mabel Fletcher TC,
South Cheshire C, Basingstoke TC, Mid-Gloucestershire
TC, Somerset CA & T, South Devon TC, Matthew
Boulton TC (Birmingham), Oswestry C, North
Lindsey CT, Fermanagh CFE, James Watt C (Greenock).

Central CCom (Glasgow). Full-time. *College Award:
certificate in creative communication.* O

London C Fashion. Full-time. *College Award: certificate
in fashion writing.* A

Chichester CT. Full-time. *College Award: certificate in
information technology.* O

Watford C. Full-time. *College Award: diploma in
advertising.* Also *diploma in advertising copywriting*

Birmingham Poly. Full-time. *College Award: diploma in
communications studies.* A

Southampton CHE. Full-time. *College Award: diploma in
creative communication studies.* A

Darlington CT. Full-time. *College Award: international
diploma in journalism*

Shirecliffe C (Sheffield). Full-time. *College Award: diploma
in media studies.* O

Redhill TC. Full-time. *College-Based: pre-vocational media
studies.* O

Retailing/Sales

Certificate Courses

Clarendon CFE (Nottingham), Thurrock TC, Distributive
Trades C, Monkwearmouth CFE, Kirkby CFE, Stoke
Cauldon CFE, Belfast CT, Central CCom (Glasgow).
Evenings. *Managing and Marketing Sales Association
Examination Board: extended diploma in salesmanship.*
P

Bedford CHE, Stoke Cauldon CFE, Central CCom
(Glasgow). Evenings. *Managing and Marketing Sales
Association Examination Board: diploma in sales
management.* O

Distributive Trades C. Full-time. *BTEC/BDSA: introduction to merchandising and display.* O

Distributive Trades C. Full-time. *BTEC: higher national diploma in business studies, fashion buying specialism.* AP

Cassio C (Watford), Wirral MC, Falmouth TC, Stoke Cauldon CFE. Block-release. *National Examinations Board for Supervisory Studies: certificate (retailing/distributive trades).* NP. Day-release at Peterborough TC, Suffolk CH & FE, Lincoln CT, North Nottinghamshire CFE, Wellingborough TC, Cassio C (Watford), Colchester I, North Hertfordshire C, Thurrock TC, Cordwainers TC, Distributive Trades C, Kingston CFE, Millbank CCom (Liverpool), St John's CFE (Manchester), Wirral MC, Oxford CFE, Falmouth TC, Gloucestershire CAT, Plymouth CFE, Swindon C, Dudley CT, Matthew Boulton TC (Birmingham), Redditch C, Stoke Cauldon CFE, Tile Hill CFE (Coventry), Wulfrun CFE (Wolverhampton), Bradford and Ilkley Community C, Dewsbury and Batley T & AC, Park Lane CFE (Leeds), Richmond CFE (Sheffield), Wakefield District C, York CA & T, Belfast CT, Central CCom (Glasgow). Evenings at North Hertfordshire C, Cordwainers TC, Havering TC (Hornchurch), Wirral MC, Swindon C, Dudley CT, Stoke Cauldon CFE, Tile Hill CFE (Coventry), Bradford and Ilkley Community C, Dewsbury and Batley T & AC, Wakefield District C, Belfast CT, Central CCom (Glasgow)

Rockingham CFE. Full-time. *Training Services Division: TOPS course in limited skills in retailing.* N

Swansea CFE. Full-time. *Training Services Division: TOPS course in salesmanship and sales office practice.* N. Block-release at Merton TC

Central CCom (Glasgow). Full-time. *College Award: certificate in fashion merchandising.* O

Distributive Trades C. Full-time. *College Award: certificate in fashion retailing.* O

Distributive Trades C. Full-time. *College Award: certificate in menswear merchandising*

Kirkby CFE. Day-release and evenings. *College Award: certificate in retailing*

Distributive Trades C, Wirral MC. Evenings. *College Award: certificate in retail salesmanship.* N

Distributive Trades C. Block- and day-release. *College Award: certificate in retail studies.* A

Central CCom (Glasgow). *College Award: preliminary certificate in fashion merchandising*

Colchester I. Full-time. *College Award: diploma in fashion retailing and display*

Falmouth TC. Full-time. *College Award: higher diploma in retailing with display endorsement.* O

Wulfrun CFE (Wolverhampton), Airedale and Wharfedale CFE. Day-release. *College-Based: unified vocational preparation course in retail work*

Marketing

CNAA Courses

Trent Poly. Sandwich. *BA(Hons) in European business.* A

Middlesex Poly. Sandwich. *BA(Hons) European business administration.* A

Buckinghamshire CHE, Hull CHE. Sandwich. *BA(Hons) in European business studies.* A

Thames Poly. Sandwich. *BA(Hons) in international marketing.* A

Bristol Poly. Full-time. *Diploma in marketing.* P

Degree Courses

City of London Poly. Full-time and day-release. *Combined subjects degree with marketing option.* A

Leicester Poly. Full-time. *Business studies degree: marketing option.* A

City of London Poly, Teesside Poly, North Staffordshire Poly. Sandwich. *Business studies degree: marketing option*

Certificate and Diploma Courses

London SAcc, London SchIns, Newcastle CA & T, West
    Bromwich CCom & T, Richmond CFE (Sheffield).
    Full-time. *Institute of Marketing qualifying certificate,
    Part I.* A. Also block-release at Kidderminster CFE.
    Day-release at Mid-Kent CH & FE, London SAcc,
    Newcastle CA & T, Blackburn CT & D, Kirkby CFE,
    North Cheshire C, St Helens CT, Salford CT, South
    Cheshire C, Slough CHE, Cornwall TC, Dorset IHE,
    Plymouth CFE, East Warwickshire CFE,
    Kidderminster CFE, Wolverhampton Poly,
    Doncaster MetIHE, Richmond CFE (Sheffield),
    Belfast CT, Central CCom (Glasgow), Dundee CCom,
    Falkirk CT, Kirkcaldy CT, Bridgend CT. Evenings at
    Luton CHE, Suffolk CH & FE, Nene C (Northampton),
    Trent Poly, Buckinghamshire CHE, Thurrock TC,
    Watford C, Brooklands TC, Mid-Kent CH & FE, City
    of London Poly, Croydon C, Distributive Trades C,
    Havering TC (Hornchurch), London SAcc, Merton TC,
    New C (Durham), Kirkby CFE, North Cheshire C,
    St John's CFE (Manchester), Salford CT, South
    Cheshire C, Stockport CT, Crawley CT,
    Farnborough CT, Highbury CT (Portsmouth),
    Slough CHE, Cornwall TC, Filton TC, Gloucestershire
    CAT, East Warwickshire CFE, Matthew Boulton TC
    (Birmingham), North Worcestershire C, Stoke
    Cauldon CFE, Sutton Coldfield CFE, Tile Hill CFE
    (Coventry), West Bromwich CCom & T,
    Wolverhampton Poly, Grimsby CT, Park Lane CFE
    (Leeds), Richmond CFE (Sheffield), York CA & T,
    Belfast CT, Newry TC, Central CCom (Glasgow),
    Dundee CCom, Falkirk CT, Kirkcaldy CT, Gwent CHE,
    South Glamorgan IGE
    All of the above feature the *Institute of Marketing
    qualifying certificate, Part II.* P
London SAcc, West Bromwich CCom & T, Belfast CT.
    Full-time. *Institute of Marketing: diploma in marketing.*
    P. Day-release at Suffolk CH & FE, Distributive
    Trades C, London SAcc, North East London Poly,

South West London C, Teesside Poly, West Cumbria C,
St Helens CT, Salford CT, Slough CHE,
Southampton CHE, Dorset IHE, North Staffordshire
Poly, West Bromwich CCom & T, Belfast CT, Dundee
CCom, Glasgow CT, Kirkcaldy CT. Evenings at
Luton CHE, Suffolk CH & FE, Leicester Poly, Nene C
(Northampton), Trent Poly, Buckinghamshire CHE,
Watford C, Mid-Kent CH & FE, City of London Poly,
Croydon C, Distributive Trades C, Ealing CHE,
Harrow CHE, London SAcc, Middlesex Poly, North East
London Poly, South Bank Poly, South West London C,
Newcastle Poly, Teesside Poly, Blackburn CT & D,
Crewe and Alsager CHE, Liverpool Poly, Manchester
Poly, Salford CT, Farnborough CT, Slough CHE, Bristol
Poly, Gloucestershire CAT, Birmingham Poly, East
Warwickshire CFE, North Staffordshire Poly, North
Worcestershire C, Stoke Cauldon CFE, West
Bromwich CCom & T, Wolverhampton Poly, Hull CHE,
Leeds Poly, Sheffield City Poly, Belfast CT,
Dundee CCom, Glasgow CT, Kirkcaldy CT, Gwent CHE

North East London Poly. Evenings. *Market Research
Society: diploma in market research.* PD

Salford CT, Hull CHE. Full-time. *BTEC: higher national
diploma in business studies, export marketing specialism.*
AP. Sandwich courses at Stockport CT, Hull CHE

Distributive Trades C, Stockport CT. Full-time. *BTEC:
higher national diploma in business studies, market
research specialism.* AP. Sandwich at Stockport CT

Buckinghamshire CHE. Full-time. *BTEC: higher national
diploma in business studies, languages and marketing
specialism.* AP. Sandwich course also available

Luton CHE, Buckinghamshire CHE, North Hertfordshire C,
Watford C, Croydon C, Distributive Trades C,
Ealing CHE, Hammersmith and West London C,
Richmond-upon-Thames C, Newcastle Poly, Teesside
Poly, Bolton IHE, Salford CT, Stockport CT,
Crawley CT, Farnborough CT, Bristol Poly, Dorset IHE,
Plymouth Poly, North Worcestershire C, Bradford and
Ilkley Community C, Huddersfield Poly, Gwent CHE,

West Glamorgan IHE. Full-time. *BTEC: higher national diploma in business studies, marketing specialism.* AP. Sandwich courses at Cambridgeshire CA & T, Luton CHE, Derby Lonsdale CHE, Buckinghamshire CHE, Ealing CHE, Thames Poly, Blackburn CT & D, Stockport CT, Crawley CT, Farnborough CT, Portsmouth Poly, North Staffordshire Poly, Poly of Wales. Day-release at Derby Lonsdale CHE, Bradford and Ilkley Community C, North East Wales IHE. Evenings at Derby Lonsdale CHE

Distributive Trades C. Evenings. *London Chamber of Commerce: marketing (Higher).* O

Thurrock TC, Distributive Trades C. Evenings. *Royal Society of Arts: commerce (marketing) Stage III.* P

Huddersfield Poly. Full-time. *College Award: diploma in marketing.* D

Huddersfield TC. Full-time. *College-Based: home and international trade management.* O

Chapter 9

Further Information

Useful Publications

Advertisers Manual — lists advertising agencies

Art and Design, Degree Course Guide, CRAC — describes subjects and compares courses

BRAD Advertisers and Agency List

The British Clothing Industry Yearbook — a classified directory of manufacturers, wholesalers and designers

Careers in Art and Design and *Jobs in the Textile and Clothing Industries* published by Kogan Page are both useful in describing jobs and careers in fashion

CNAA Directory — lists CNAA degree courses

Creative Handbook — lists design consultancies and advertising agencies

Design Courses in Britain — printed twice a year by the Design Council, lists all BA, vocational and advanced courses

Directory of First Degree and DipHE Courses — lists courses and describes application procedure

Directory of Further Education, CRAC

Graduate Studies, CRAC — summarises postgraduate courses

Institute of Public Relations Members' Register

Marketing Yearbook

UCCA Handbook — a guide to university degree courses

Which Degree?, Haymarket Press — summarises courses at universities, colleges and polytechnics

Writers' and Artists' Yearbook — lists publishers and photographic agencies

You may also consult any relevant career leaflets obtainable from Careers and Occupational Information Centre (COIC) or found in school and careers libraries, and leaflets from the Arts Council and the Crafts Council.

Journals Containing Job Vacancies

Advertisers' Weekly
British Clothing Manufacturer
Campaign
Clothing and Footwear Journal
Design
Designer
Drapers' Record
Fashion Weekly
Illustration
Manufacturing Clothier
UK Press Gazette

Helpful Organisations

Advertising Association, Abford House, 15 Wilton Street, London SW1

Association of Cinematograph, Televison and Allied Technicians, 2 Soho Square, London W1

Association of Fashion, Advertising and Editorial Photographers, 10a Dryden Street, London WC2E 9NA

Association of Illustrators, 17 Carlton House Terrace, London SW1

British Institute of Professional Photography, Amwell End, Ware, Hertfordshire

Bureau of Freelance Photographers, Steward House, 59 Tottenham Lane, London N8

Careers and Occupational Information Centre, Department CW, Moorfoot, Sheffield S1 4PQ

Central Services Unit for Careers and Appointment Services, Crawford House, Precinct Centre, Oxford Road, Manchester

Clothing and Allied Products Industry Training Board, Tower House, Merrion Way, Leeds

Clothing and Footwear Institute, 71 Brushfield Street,
    London E1 6AA
Textile Institute, 10 Blackfriars Street, Manchester

Arts Council, 105 Piccadilly, London W1
Crafts Council, 8 Waterloo Place, London SW1
Design Council, The Design Centre, 28 Haymarket,
    London SW1
Scottish Arts Council, 19 Charlotte Street, Edinburgh